African-Americans and the Doctoral Experience

Implications for Policy

African-Americans and the Doctoral Experience

Implications for Policy

CHARLES V. WILLIE
MICHAEL K. GRADY
RICHARD O. HOPE

Teachers College, Columbia University
New York and London

Published by Teachers College Press, 1234 Amsterdam Avenue,
New York, NY 10027

Library of Congress Cataloging-in-Publication Data

Willie, Charles Vert, 1927–
    African-Americans and the doctoral experience : implications for
policy / Charles V. Willie, Michael K. Grady, Richard O. Hope.
        p.   cm.
    Includes bibliographical references and index.
    ISBN 0-8077-3087-4 (alk. paper)
    1. Afro-Americans—Education (Higher)—Longitudinal studies.
    2. Afro-American college students—Longitudinal studies.
    3. Universities and colleges—United States—Graduate work.   4. Afro-
American universities and colleges—Graduate work.
    5. Scholarships.   6. Doctor of philosophy degree—United States.
    7. Educational surveys—United States.   I. Grady, Michael K.
    II. Hope, Richard O.   III. Title.
    LC2781.W55   1991
    378.1'98296073—dc20   90-26351
                                                                          CIP

ISBN 0-8077-3087-4

Printed on acid-free paper
Manufactured in the United States of America

98 97 96 95 94 93 92 91   8 7 6 5 4 3 2 1

Contents

Preface

The 1980s were an anomaly in higher education. A greater proportion of blacks had graduated from college during the 1970s than in earlier decades, and their indicators of competence increased during this period. However, the proportion of blacks in graduate school during the 1980s decreased from the proportion in post-college educational programs during the previous decade.

This study attempts to shed light on this phenomenon by examining a highly motivated group of 146 black scholars who pursued graduate education between 1977 and 1985. All were faculty members at United Negro College Fund (UNCF) institutions when they were awarded grants by the Lilly Endowment to pursue full-time study.

To provide a context for this study, Chapter 1 examines trends in the participation of blacks in higher education, and Chapter 2 reviews the development of black colleges and the growth of the United Negro College Fund. In Chapter 3 we describe how we gathered data for our study and review pertinent research literature. The instruments used in gathering data are found in the Appendixes. In the remaining chapters we analyze the possible association between fellowship amount, duration of funding, and degree-completion rate. The campus as a social context for black graduate students is also examined. A unique aspect of this study is its investigation in a comparative way of the adaptations made by black graduate students to predominantly white and to predominantly black graduate schools. It examines not only the campus as a learning environment but also the mentoring roles that professors perform and whether apprenticeship opportunities such as teaching assistantships and research assistantships are available to black graduate students.

The findings of this investigation indicate that the provision of ample fellowship support is an effective way of increasing the number of blacks with doctoral degrees. Because this study discovers factors that are likely to affect the rate of degree-completion, it should be of great interest to policy makers in philanthropy and in the federal government and to organizers of academic programs in higher education, as well as to college and university administrators and educators who are interested in education and in effectively managing it.

Acknowledgments

The Lilly Endowment has had a long-standing interest in increasing opportunities among American minorities to obtain graduate degrees. We are grateful for the support of William Bonifield, who commissioned this study on behalf of Lilly, and to Glegg Watson of the Xerox Foundation, who recognized its value. The Xerox Foundation awarded a grant to the W. E. B. DuBois Institute for Afro-American Research at Harvard University and to the Harvard Graduate School of Education so that analysis of the data could be completed and presented in book form. Lea Williams, who served as Assistant Director of Educational Services of the United Negro College Fund when this study began, was of inestimable help, as was James Smothers, Jr., then UNCF Educational Services Director.

Acknowledged with appreciation is the expert editorial and clerical assistance rendered by Susan Liddicoat, Myra Cleary, and Kathy George.

African-Americans and the Doctoral Experience

Implications for Policy

1 Trends in Blacks' Participation in Higher Education

Harvard College was established in 1636 and represented the beginning of formal and organized concern with providing higher education for the people of North America on their own continent. Nearly two centuries would pass before a black would obtain a college degree from an institution of higher education in the United States. The first college degree awarded to an African-American person in this nation was in 1826.[1] A quarter of a century later, Lincoln University in Pennsylvania (beginning as Ashmun Institute in 1854) and Wilberforce University in Ohio (incorporated in 1856, although fund raising for its establishment began in 1855) became the first institutions devoted to the higher education of blacks in the United States that have remained in existence until the present period of time (Franklin, 1967). (See Chapter 2 for further information on the development of black colleges.)

BLACK ENROLLMENT

Before the beginning of the twentieth century, only 2,079 blacks are recorded as having graduated from college, according to W.E.B. DuBois (cited in Franklin, 1967). DuBois received a doctoral degree from Harvard University in 1895. His was a unique achievement for an African-American scholar of that time. With the exception of Harvard, the University of Wisconsin, Yale, and a few other universities, "blacks could not receive [graduate] professional training at most historically white institutions" (Blackwell, 1987, p. 7). Historian John Hope Franklin reports, for example, that only 57 doctorates were

---

1. The terms *black* and *African-American* are used interchangeably throughout this book.

conferred on blacks during the decade of the Depression (1930–39; cited in Blackwell, 1987). This was the decade when the National Association for the Advancement of Colored People (NAACP) began in earnest its work to gain admissions to graduate and professional schools for blacks (Blackwell, 1987).

Until the midpoint of the twentieth century the best chance for graduate professional education for blacks was found in institutions established specifically for their population. As late as 1968, the year in which Martin Luther King, Jr., died, 80% of black physicians and dentists were graduates of Meharry Medical College and Howard University, two historically black schools. According to James Blackwell (1987), "no historically black college offered a doctoral degree [in a discipline of the arts and sciences] . . . before 1954" (p. 7). Thus the opportunity for blacks to obtain doctoral degrees is a phenomenon limited largely to the second half of the twentieth century.

In 1950, before the *Brown* decision of the Supreme Court, which declared segregated education to be unlawful, only 2.2% of blacks and other minority races over 25 years of age had graduated from college; toward the end of the century (in 1988), the proportion has dramatically increased to 16.4% (National Center for Educational Statistics, 1988b). Meanwhile, the proportion of white college graduates at the midpoint of the twentieth century (6.6%) was 3 times greater than the proportion of blacks and other races who had achieved this level of schooling. Toward the end of the century (in 1988), however, the proportion of white college graduates, 20.9%, was only 1.3 times greater than that of blacks and other races, which was 16.4% (National Center for Educational Statistics, 1989b). For African-Americans alone, the proportion that had graduated from college as this century moved from its midpoint (in 1950) toward the final decades (in 1986) increased from less than 2% to approximately 12% (National Center for Educational Statistics, 1988b).

Over the years in the United States, the enrollment of blacks in higher education has been a most sensitive indicator of their economic circumstances, on the one hand, and social or public policy to compensate for their inadequate resources, on the other. The educational aspirations of blacks have always been high. Surveys reveal that a higher proportion of blacks compared with whites believe that a college education is "very important" (U.S. Bureau of the Census, 1980). Nevertheless, the proportion of whites 25 years and older who received a college education has been continuously higher than the proportion of blacks of these ages who have received this level of education. This was true of the two racial populations before the *Brown* decision in 1954 and continues to be their experience into the final decades of this century.

EFFECTS OF FINANCIAL AID POLICIES

After the death of Martin Luther King, Jr., the nation began to make an appropriate response to challenges by blacks for equal educational opportunities. The middle years of the 1970s are identified as the apex of racial inclusiveness in higher education in this country. By 1978, the proportion of blacks over 25 years of age who had studied in programs of graduate education had increased to 3.1% from 1.3% in 1968 (U.S. Bureau of the Census, 1980).

However, in 1978, Public Law 95–566 modified the provisions for student financial aid to allow middle income students to qualify for federal educational assistance. This action represented a pullback by the federal government from more or less exclusive concern for disadvantaged populations. In 1983, Title III of the Higher Education Act was amended in a way that encouraged institutions to seek alternative sources of funding; such alternatives were not readily available to historically black institutions. The outcome of these and other changes was a shift in federal government student aid from grants to loans. Grants, of course, favored lower income students, and loans were targeted at students from middle income families (National Center for Educational Statistics, 1988a).

During the 1970s and 1980s the median family income of blacks in constant dollars lagged one-fourth to one-third behind that of whites. Indeed, the 1986 median family income of blacks in constant dollars was nearly $300 less than the 1975 median, while that for whites increased about 6% during this period (National Center for Educational Statistics, 1989c). The American Council on Education reports that between 1976 and 1987, the number of African-Americans earning bachelor's degrees fell 4.3%; the number earning master's degrees decreased by 31.8%; and the number earning Ph.D. degrees between 1977 and 1988 declined 21% (Carter & Wilson, 1989). These figures indicate how sensitive the degree-completion rate is to economic circumstances among blacks.

The American Council on Education explains that "student aid . . . had a good deal to do with the upswing in college participation . . . by African-Americans," for "during the mid-1970s . . . the

Pell Grant program reached its highest funding level" (Carter & Wilson, 1989, p. 8). Reginald Wilson's analysis (cited in Willie, 1989a) of this phenomenon is straightforward:

1. "College enrollment for minority groups is related to family financial status" (p. 1).
2. The poverty of black people limits their capacity to educate their children.
3. When resources external to family finances are available to them, more blacks go to college.

Based on this analysis, we question the usefulness of the social policies advocated by William Wilson (1987), which are against group-specific approaches to social reforms. Wilson has advocated programs of economic and social reform that are seen as "universal" by the general public. In other words, the agenda of policy makers who wish to improve the life chances of disadvantaged groups, according to Wilson, should be one that emphasizes "programs to which the more advantaged groups of all races and class backgrounds can positively relate" (p. 154). Wilson believes that "it is imperative that the political message underline the need for economic and social reforms that benefit all groups in the United States, not just poor minorities" (p. 155).

By 1978, the federal government began to implement a policy that is similar to that advocated by Wilson. As noted, middle income as well as low income students were allowed to qualify for federal education assistance. By 1985 federal funds obligated for guaranteed student loans were larger in amount than the quantity of funds obligated for educational opportunity grants. The guaranteed student loan obligation was only about one-third of all federal funds for postsecondary student financial assistance in 1980, shortly after Congress had authorized the participation of middle income students in this student-assistance program. In just 5 years this program had obligated nearly one-half of the federal funds for student assistance. By 1989, one-fifth of $20.6 billion spent by the U.S. Department of Education went to banks to subsidize student loans, but only one-sixth went to college students (National Center for Educational Statistics, 1989a).

This analysis demonstrates that when a group-specific program was broadened to accommodate "the more advantaged groups of all races and class backgrounds," as recommended by William Wilson, it may have gained support from a wider population but also drew support away from the disadvantaged. The declining number of African-Americans awarded doctorates has been an unfortunate outcome of this "universal," nonrace-specific, nonclass-specific policy.

Modifications in federal student aid policies that began in 1978 broke the production trend of more than 1,000 blacks annually who received Ph.D. degrees between 1978 and 1982 and started a downward plunge in the annual trend that has produced blacks with Ph.D. degrees at less than 1,000 a year for the remainder of the 1980s. In 1988, only 805 African-Americans were awarded Ph.D. degrees compared with 1,033 who received such degrees in 1978 (Carter & Wilson, 1989), the year in which the federal government began to broaden the category of income groups eligible for student assistance. Thus, a broadened income range of students eligible for federal student aid ultimately was harmful to those from lower income groups who depended on federal government help and did not have alternative sources of support.

ACADEMIC COMPETENCE OF BLACK STUDENTS

Evidence that the trend of declining participation of blacks in higher education is a function of their disadvantaged economic circumstances and the absence of compensating social policies of redress is revealed in studies of the increasing competence of black high school and college graduates. These students demonstrate that blacks today are not less able than in the past. *Black Issues in Higher Education* reports that "all minority groups have experienced long-term gains" in scores on college entrance examinations (O'Brien, 1989, p. 1). For example, in 1980 the average verbal score for blacks on the College Board Scholastic Aptitude Test was 330; 9 years later, this score was 351. On the mathematical score, the average for blacks was 360 in 1980 and 386 in 1989. The increase was 21 and 26 points, respectively. Scores for blacks on the Graduate Record Examination have increased too. While such test scores are of doubtful validity as indicators of the capacity of blacks to perform academic tasks adequately and effectively, they nevertheless demonstrate that the declining enrollment of blacks in graduate schools must be due to factors other than declining test scores.

"A major part of the educational reform movement," according to the U.S. Department of Education, "has been [the encouragement of] students to take . . . an increased number of basic courses in English, social studies, and mathematics" (National Center for Educational Statistics, 1989a, p. 22). The record reveals that in the period between 1982 and 1987, the percentage of students who completed 4 credits in English, and 3 each in social studies, science, and mathematics has doubled. "The increase was shared by all racial and ethnic groups," reports the Department of Education (p. 22). For example, only 10% of black high school graduates earned credits in these courses in 1982. But 24% earned such credits in 1987. Again there is no evidence of retrogression in competence on the part of minorities that may explain their declining rate of participation in higher education during the closing decades of the twentieth century.

James Blackwell's analysis of happenings in medical college admissions is a fitting summary to this discussion of trends of the participation of blacks in higher education. He states that "the admission of black students to medical college is declining even though their test scores and other indices of eligibility are improving" (cited in Willie, 1989a, p. 7). This finding is a puzzlement that caused Blackwell to wonder if the graduate and professional schools of this nation are interested in developing the pool of talent among African-Americans.

CONCLUSIONS

The compensation of blacks and other minorities for the insufficient financial resources that have impeded their college and graduate school studies is a way of implementing the principle of redress, an essential social policy in any society that aspires to be fair to all. The principle of redress has a better chance of fulfilling the requirements of equality regarding the participation of blacks in higher education, especially graduate school education, if it favors grant programs over loan programs. One reason for favoring grants over loans as a method of redress is the dissimilar income that minorities tend to receive compared with whites for performing similar work. For example,

> Poorly educated blacks in 1982 earned 23% less than the [median] income received by poorly educated whites. The same pattern persisted for highly educated blacks who are college graduates; they earned 22% less than the [median] income received by highly educated whites; . . . inequity that is racially based remains. (Willie, 1989b, p. 88)

An analysis of full-time workers who are 25 to 34 years of age reveals that in 1988 blacks with 4 or more years of college education had a median income that was almost the same as that of whites who were college dropouts (National Center for Educational Statistics, 1989c). Because of the continuation of racial discrimination in the United States, education does not do as much for blacks as it does for whites in terms of income received. Thus, more grants should be available for blacks who wish to participate in higher education, since they cannot recover the costs of higher education from income as quickly as whites can. The principle of redress requires a revision of the policy of favoring loans over grants in financial programs for racial minorities.

The declining participation of black men and women at all levels of higher education has heightened the urgency for a coordinated political and institutional response. Given the striking underrepresentation of blacks with doctorates, declining enrollment in colleges and universities, and demographic projections, we believe it should be a federal priority to increase the graduation rate of minority graduate students. Likewise, major research institutions that seek to enroll black candidates for advanced degrees must develop effective strategies to increase the success rate of these candidates. This can be done by providing minority students with adequate forms of academic, social, and financial support. Finally, current or prospective candidates for advanced degrees must fully anticipate the personal and professional challenges of graduate study and the unique challenges of minority scholars within the majority academic setting. The following study is directed to these audiences and all other groups and individuals who are committed to promoting success among those black men and women who aspire to join the community of scholars.

2 Development of the Black Colleges

The experience of African-Americans in higher education prior to the Emancipation Proclamation was limited largely to the North. It is reported that 28 blacks graduated from northern colleges before the Civil War. In most instances, these individuals were trained for missionary work in Africa. Others involved free blacks who were preparing for teaching or religious careers in border states.

In the immediate aftermath of the Civil War, a few black colleges were founded, primarily by Christian missionaries in the North. According to Jane Smith Browning and John Williams (1978), "by and large, the missionaries tended to mix social, economic and religious ideas in their dedication to the task of uplifting the freed men and women" (p. 69).

In large part, these colleges survived due to the effort and philanthropy of Christian missionaries. The mission of the black college was constrained by local political and educational leadership in the South, which remained "ambivalent about the intellectual heights to which [blacks] should be encouraged to rise" (Fleming, 1984, p. 5).

By 1880, the emphasis in several black colleges had shifted from liberal arts education to vocational education. Ten years later the Morrill Act required state systems of higher education to provide either separate institutions for blacks or access to mainstream white colleges and universities. Southern state legislatures, which since the late 1870s had been dominated by segregationists intent on restoring antebellum social codes and mores, opted for separate facilities for black college students. These were, with few exceptions, "teacher training schools for black women; . . . the majority of black public colleges, then, evolved out of states' desires to avoid admitting blacks to existing white institutions and facilities provided were accordingly inferior" (Fleming, 1984, p. 5).

EVOLUTION OF THE BLACK COLLEGE MISSION

The legitimacy of the vocational focus of these institutions was challenged at the turn of the century by scholars who believed in broader academic programs. As Jacqueline Fleming (1984) has noted,

> While both forms of education managed to co-exist, disproportionate amounts of public funds were channeled into vocational institutions. Thus, a financial strategy successfully forced [many black] colleges into the role of non-intellectual institutions. (p. 6)

This tension between vocational and liberal arts educations was embodied in the debate between W. E. B. DuBois and Booker T. Washington (see Willie & Edmonds, 1978, for further discussion of the debate).

Alternatives to the vocational training centers began to emerge in the early twentieth century. Popularly coined the Black Ivy League, schools such as Morehouse, Spelman, and Fisk restored liberal arts as the central focus of academic programs at black colleges.

According to Fleming (1984), surveys conducted in the 1920s constituted the first serious attempts to document the quality of education in the black colleges. These investigations found "many of them, and especially the private liberal arts colleges, worthy of accreditation alongside mainstream American colleges" (p. 7).

IMPACT OF THE CIVIL RIGHTS MOVEMENT
AND OTHER RECENT DEVELOPMENTS

Fleming (1984) reported that some people have questioned whether black colleges and universities should continue to exist. She examined the main question underlying this debate: Do black colleges serve a worthwhile purpose in the context of modern life? Because several black colleges are resource-poor, some critics have labeled them as "anachronisms in contemporary society [that] have outlived their usefulness" (p. 1). Other observers, however, understand the unique, vital contribution of the traditionally black college to American society. Daniel Thompson (1973) reports that graduates of these institutions are prepared to compete as equals in a very complex industrial society.

To fulfill their missions, black colleges and universities need competent faculties. Fleming (1984) identifies the key factors that could enhance retention of good faculty:

1. Offering salaries that are comparable to other colleges and universities
2. Assuring young scholars of academic and professional growth
3. Providing a climate in which faculty are confident that they are rendering worthy and respected professional services

Patricia Gurin and Edgar Epps (1975) argue that "several dangers [exist for] traditionally black colleges," including the possibility that these institutions could be "desegregated out of existence" (p. 29). This is ironic, they believe, because "some of these schools have never excluded white students" (p. 30); moreover, all have had and continue to operate with a high level of racial and ethnic diversity among faculty and administrators.

In 1950, 90% of black students in higher education were served in traditionally black colleges. By 1967, 3 years after the Civil Rights Act of 1964, 75% of blacks were enrolled in traditionally white institutions. Yet due to high attrition rates of blacks at white institutions during this same period, 80% of blacks earning baccalaureate degrees at that time were graduates of black colleges.

Additional evidence of the importance of black colleges in developing the black community was presented in the mid-1970s by Butler Jones (1974). He reported that 75% of all black Ph.D.s, 75% of black army officers, 80% of black federal judges, and 85% of black physicians were graduates of black colleges. Fleming (1975) cites Benjamin Mays' belief that "virtually all of the leaders instrumental in solving the problems of race relations in America trace their roots to black institutions" (p. 9). Earl McGrath (1965) found that strong psychological and social factors cause many African-Americans to gravitate toward black colleges. Fleming (1984) explains that "black colleges afford more opportunities for black students to assume leadership roles . . . thereby providing them with a rehearsal for the roles they are expecting to assume in society" (p. 152). Such opportunities are likely to be "frustrating" on predominantly white campuses, according to Fleming.

The capacity of the historically black colleges to foster persistence among their students was still evident in 1975 when 85 black institutions enrolled 42% of black undergraduates but granted 70% of college degrees conferred to black candidates.

A study conducted by Charles Willie and Marlene MacLeish

(1978) revealed that many black colleges view as a vital part of their mission

> giving supportive services to those students whose academic backgrounds reflect low levels of achievement, reopening the doors which have been closed to many students, [providing] catch-up academic programs for underprepared freshmen, reaching students where they are, enroll[ing] students who are not typically thought of as college material, [and giving students] the inspiration and goading they need to maximize their potential. (pp. 138–139)

Harvard-educated John Monro (1978), who has amassed decades of experience in black colleges, stated that half of the entering class in one college where he taught read at or below the ninth-grade level and two-thirds were among the bottom 10% in mathematical skills as measured by standardized achievement tests. Yet, with care and concern, Monro and others developed first-year courses that enabled half of the entering class to survive in college and a significant "percentage to obtain honors" (p. 247). To accomplish these results, Monro believes that a school needs "dedicated faculty who are interested in teaching students, rather than just teaching a subject" (p. 236). Many black colleges recruit such faculty and perform these functions; yet, Monro has observed that "most [other] colleges do not see this effort as part of their responsibility" (p. 236).

Many speak in favorable terms for continued support of the black college in the modern life of higher education. Gurin and Epps (1975) propose that the existence of these institutions is especially important for the improvement of educational opportunities for black students in the South, "where historical conditions have limited Black opportunities at all levels of the educational system" (p. 24).

The validity of predominantly black institutions, especially during the 1980s, has come under greater scrutiny from several sources. In the words of Fleming (1984), these "schools are increasingly asked to justify their continued existence" (p. 24).

Black colleges are facing several key challenges to their institutional solvency. Some colleges are operating in profound states of poverty; a few have succumbed and had to close during the past decade. Located in isolated rural areas of the South, some black colleges have been challenged by growth of urban commuter schools and demographic trends. Exigencies that restrict student recruitment, such as institutional poverty and geography, affect faculty development as well.

THE UNITED NEGRO COLLEGE FUND

The United Negro College Fund (UNCF) represents a consortium of 43 predominantly black colleges and universities. All schools are private and fully accredited. In 1985 the 43 colleges and universities served an enrollment of over 45,000 students. The principal mission of the UNCF is to assist the member institutions in raising revenue for basic operations.

Historical Background

The UNCF was founded in 1943. During the early years of the Fund, a majority of the black students receiving baccalaureate degrees came from predominantly black colleges. Unlike many other private institutions, most historically black colleges had only modest endowments and could not rely on such earnings to provide needed funds to supplement their tuition revenue, which remained low to accommodate the limited income of their students. Alumni contributions also had been minimal.

Two factors mitigated against external support. First, there was a gradual decline in foundation and church giving. Second, some foundations attempted to work "within the framework and traditions of the South" (Wolters, 1975, p. 8); financial support often was awarded to black colleges on the condition that they concentrate on teacher training and vocational education, which were perceived as more appropriate for blacks at that time.

Church-related colleges did receive funding from their church boards; however, contributions tended to be small relative to the total financial needs and the numbers of institutions seeking funding. Also, independent fund-raising efforts tended to yield modest results.

Out of this crisis of support for predominantly black colleges and universities came the following statement that changed the course of history for these institutions:

> Negro institutions may well take a cue from . . . most charitable efforts today. Various and sundry drives are being unified . . . in behalf of a more purposeful and pointed approach to the giving public. It seems most propitious at this time that the several institutions referred to, pool the small monies which they are spending for campaign and publicity and that they make a unified appeal to national conscience. (Patterson, 1943)

Put forth by Frederick Patterson, president of Tuskegee Institute, this idea became known as the Patterson Plan. On April 19, 1943, 14 presidents of black institutions met together at Tuskegee Institute to explore ways of implementing this plan. By September 1943, the number of participating colleges grew to 27 on the promise of foundation support from the General Education Board and the Rosenwald Fund.

Another meeting occurred at Atlanta University, where such questions as membership and criteria for membership were discussed. The decision was to include only those institutions that by that time had met the educational standards set by the proper accrediting agencies of their region. Only in this way, they felt, could the public be assured of the quality of the institutions. It was agreed, too, that all must be tax-exempt, privately supported 4-year colleges or professional schools. By April 1944 the United Negro College Fund was incorporated under the laws of New York State. Its stated mission was to aid the cause of higher education for "members of the Negro people" in the United States. The article of incorporation continues by describing its modus operandi as aiding the cause of Negro higher education "by conducting solicitation and campaigns . . . for the benefit and aid of colleges and similar institutions of higher education . . . availed by members of the Negro people" (By-Laws of the United Negro College Fund, Inc., Albany, NY; April 25, 1944; art. 2, p. 1).

Operation

In the first year of its incorporation, the UNCF received funds totaling $765,000. As evident from Table 2.1, the UNCF has made

TABLE 2.1 UNCF Fund-raising Sources for 1944 and 1987

Source	1944		1987	
	$	%	$	%
Individual	$332,000	43.4	$13,064,103	32.8
Corporate	228,000	29.8	11,785,362	29.6
Foundation	163,000	21.3	4,930,273	12.4
Other	42,000	5.5	10,038,651	25.2
Total	765,000	100.0	39,818,389	100.0

significant strides in its fund raising. However, fund raising is only one part of its important contribution to its members. Lea Williams, assistant director of educational services, describes three other key components to the UNCF operation as public relations, advocacy, and research.

In its advocacy role, the UNCF's Washington, DC, office disseminates information to the colleges and to Congress; the organization maintains regular contact with the Congressional Black Caucus and local, state, and federal government agencies.

The UNCF has a research department that regularly responds to requests for data and their analysis. It also assists in fund-raising activities by maintaining records on contributors, investments, expenditures, and so forth.

Member Colleges

Forty-two United Negro College Fund institutions operate in 11 southern states, stretching from Virginia to Texas; the forty-third institution is located in the state of Ohio. The heaviest concentration of UNCF colleges is in the states of Georgia (7), North Carolina (6), Texas (6), and Alabama (5). These states account for 56% of all UNCF institutions. Approximately two-thirds of the colleges are located in urban areas with populations in excess of 50,000. Of this group, six are in the Atlanta metropolitan area.

Enrollments at UNCF institutions are comparatively small by national higher education standards, as seen in Table 2.2. Information provided by a sample of UNCF college presidents indicates an average

TABLE 2.2 General Characteristics of UNCF Institutions

Descriptor	Enrollment	Budget (millions)	Full-time Faculty
Mean	1014.5	$ 9.2	65.8
Standard Deviation	618.9	7.7	49.9
Minimum Value	300.0	2.5	24.0
Median Value	787.0	6.6	52.0
Maximum Value	3400.0	45.0	300.0

Note. Number of responding institutions = 30 (enrollment, full-time faculty); 29 (budget).

enrollment slightly in excess of 1,000 full-time equivalent students. However, the range of enrollment figures for individual colleges is quite broad, with the largest supporting 3,400 students and the smallest, 300.

A range of financial conditions is also evident based on a review of the variation in budget data of the institutions, as seen in Table 2.2. The average budget for a UNCF college in 1985 was $9.2 million. This average shrinks considerably if the largest college budget (which is two-and-one-half times that of the second largest budget) is eliminated from the sample. When the impact of this institution is eliminated, UNCF colleges collectively had a median budget of only $6.6 million.

Table 2.2 also shows that faculties at UNCF colleges range from a maximum of 300 to a minimum of 24 full-time teachers. The median number of instructors on UNCF faculties is 52.

An analysis of the racial, ethnic, and gender compositions of UNCF faculties presents a rich profile of cultural diversity, as seen in Table 2.3. A majority of faculty at UNCF colleges are men. However, females make up 44% of the total full-time teaching staff at UNCF institutions. Similarly, the colleges support a racially integrated teaching faculty: 63% black, 27% white, and 10% foreign born.

College presidents report that roughly 53% of the instructional staff holds doctoral degrees, as seen in Table 2.4. Again, there is a substantial range among UNCF colleges for this institutional characteristic. Eighty-four percent of teachers had doctorates at the college with the highest proportion of professors with doctoral degrees; the lowest ranking college in this respect supported a faculty of which slightly less than one-fourth (24%) had earned the terminal degree.

TABLE 2.3 Racial and Sex Characteristics of UNCF Faculty

Descriptors	Race			Sex	
	Black	White	Other	Male	Female
Mean	63.0%	26.8%	10.2%	56.2%	43.8%
Standard Deviation	14.7	13.1	8.8	11.4	11.4
Minimum Value	20.0%	5.0%	0.0%	25.0%	13.0%
Median Value	60.0%	26.0%	12.0%	57.0%	43.0%
Maximum Value	90.0%	50.0%	30.0%	87.0%	75.0%

Note. Number of responding institutions = 27.

TABLE 2.4 Actual versus Preferred Percentage of Earned Doctorates on UNCF Faculties (According to UNCF Presidents)

Descriptor	Actual	Preferred
Mean	53.2%	72.9%
Standard Deviation	14.5	15.8
Minimum Value	24.0%	35.0%
Median Value	50.0%	70.0%
Maximum Value	84.0%	100.0%

Note. Number of responding institutions = 30 (actual); 28 (preferred).

STRENGTHENING FACULTIES IN BLACK COLLEGES

Perhaps the least known and one of the most important functions of the UNCF is its assistance in the recruitment and retention of faculty for member institutions. It does this, in part, by soliciting funds for faculty development programs. Although an average of 53% of institutional staff at UNCF colleges held a doctorate, the presidents indicated that the optimal proportion of doctoral-degree faculty was approximately three-fourths (72.9%).

The Lilly Endowment has demonstrated a commitment for several years in faculty development programs for black colleges. A grant of $140,000 for this and other purposes was made to the UNCF in 1973 for distribution to its member institutions. Lilly Endowment's expectation was that this and subsequent grants would expand opportunities for individuals who may otherwise be excluded according to a memorandum prepared for its Board of Trustees. During the initial years of the grant program the goal was oriented more to expanding opportunities than providing scholarship assistance. Under the rubric of "expansion of opportunities," Lilly included professional enrichment conferences and faculty merit awards as well as some scholarship assistance.

By 1974, the case for faculty scholarship aid had been effectively articulated by the United Negro College Fund. Lilly authorized a grant of $240,000, 60% of which was for the purpose of assisting UNCF faculty members to obtain doctoral degrees. The Lilly-sponsored faculty development program that we have evaluated began with this grant. The program required grant recipients to pursue a full-time program of graduate study during a 10–12 month period. Faculty scholars were obligated to return to their institution of employment for at least two years following their period of study.

By 1976, the Lilly Endowment and the United Negro College Fund had refined the focus of the program. It clearly was to be a faculty development program with grants made directly to individuals to take leaves of absence from regular campus responsibilities to work full time on completing requirements for a doctoral degree. Faculty members were eligible for renewal awards. But, by practice, they were limited to one renewal and seldom to two or more. Only one-third of the faculty scholars received renewal grants. The program was intended for the full range of UNCF institutions—those with strong departments in which faculty with doctoral degrees would enhance their positions in higher education in general, and weaker departments that needed upgrading.

The Lilly Endowment phased out its general support to the United Negro College Fund in 1977 but continued funding for the faculty development program. That funding continued through the 1980s in sums ranging annually from $200,000 to $360,000.

Recognizing the importance of a fully credentialed faculty, several other foundations and corporations have provided faculty development programs in which UNCF institutions have participated. Danforth, Ford, Rockefeller, and Mellon foundations and businesses like Citicorp, for example, have provided fellowship assistance to experienced and mid-career professionals connected with predominantly black and other minority-oriented institutions (Rockefeller Foundation, 1977). In addition to blacks, these fellowship programs have supported Hispanics and Native Americans. These educational assistance programs specifically targeted to minority populations have been of great assistance, largely because they were targeted.

Private foundation and corporation support has been significant for faculty development programs because historically black colleges (and especially UNCF institutions) received little financial support from governmental sources before passage of the 1965 Higher Education Act; and even this public support diminished quickly during the first decade of its existence.

Darryl Brown, in the February 1986 issue of *Youth Policy*, states that Title III funds of the Higher Education Act were for the purpose of "strengthening endowments and other aspects of historically black colleges" but that such institutions increasingly have been "pushed out of the competition for the federal money . . . [by] other colleges and universities" (p. 8). In the early 1980s, only 58% of the historically black colleges received Title III funds; 42% with low endowments had to look for assistance elsewhere. Despite the fact that Title III funds, according to Brown, were intended "to alleviate the fiscal hardships of historically black colleges, such schools received only about one-third of Title III funds in the early 1980s" (p. 8). Thus, the need for support targeted to UNCF and other historically black and minority-oriented institutions remains.

The Lilly/UNCF Faculty Development Program and those of other foundations and corporations have been well received by the presidents of historically black institutions. When presidents of UNCF colleges were asked to project the future demand for support for faculty development, 96% (or all but one in the sample) expressed an interest in participating in a faculty development program like the Lilly/UNCF program in future years. This takes on added significance when considered with the fact that five presidents who indicated interest represented schools that had not previously participated in the program. This finding suggests that faculty development programs have gained almost universal acceptance among private black colleges and universities.

Upon indicating an interest in the program, the presidents were asked to estimate the number of faculty members who might apply for support in a typical future year. The presidents estimated that in any given year an average of 2.4 faculty members per institution might participate in a faculty development program like the Lilly/UNCF program. The UNCF colleges need about 100 faculty development scholarships a year to fulfill the quality needs identified by their presidents. This study will demonstrate the importance of continuing faculty development programs targeted to African-American and other racial and ethnic groups and will indicate modifications that may make such programs more effective.

3 Data and Methods of the Study

A major challenge facing the leading institutions of higher education is to increase the number of minority scholars on their faculties. This can be accomplished only through well-conceived recruitment and retention programs. As part of the process of reaching this goal, there must be expansion in the pool of minority graduate students completing requirements for their doctorates. This study of one program for graduate scholars provides insight into those experiences that serve as facilitators and as barriers to graduate degree completion for blacks. The results of this study have important implications for higher education policy.

Obtaining the doctorate by black scholars has always been heralded as a major and singular achievement because it marks three important events. First, it represents personal success, working against significant odds such as poverty, racism, and competing pressures to accept lesser career opportunities and training to satisfy more immediate needs. Second, the attainment of the doctorate has symbolized for the African-American community in general group attainment within the larger society. Third, a doctoral degree can be viewed as a barometer or index of national strength. As the twenty-first century approaches with its increasing requirements for greater scientific knowledge, the production of scientists for teaching, research, and administration must be considered a major national priority. According to demographic projections, one-third of the work force in the United States will be minority by the year 2000. Minorities will be needed increasingly to occupy positions in the scientific community that were filled primarily by white males. It can be argued that the production of doctoral degrees among blacks is an indicator of the potential strength of the United States as a world power in science and technology.

As pointed out in Chapter 1, recent trends are not promising, for there is evidence of retrogression in the production of doctoral degrees among minorities. Analyzed by career fields, the situation is even worse—particularly in the mathematics, science, and engineering

19

fields. These represent fields of specialization of greatest decline and, at the same time, probably of greatest need in the next century.

Even though white males have dominated in the rate of doctorates produced, it is clear that a declining white birthrate will reduce future strength. Population trends suggest that African-Americans and Hispanics will significantly outdistance the birthrates of the white population in the near future. Therefore, scientists, engineers, social scientists, mathematicians, and other scholars increasingly must come from the ranks of the racial and ethnic minority populations.

ISSUES EXAMINED IN THE STUDY

As explained in Chapter 2, the Lilly Endowment sponsored a faculty development program through the United Negro College Fund for UNCF member institutions. The goal of the program was to assist faculty members in private black colleges obtain doctoral degrees and become fully credentialed scholars.

The Lilly Endowment commissioned an evaluation of this program in 1985 to determine its effectiveness. Preliminary findings were presented to Lilly in a report in October 1985 (Willie, Grady, & Hope, 1985). The rest of the chapters in this book brings together data presented in the report, further analyzes them, arrives at conclusions, and discusses their implications.

Data are provided on important background factors, including the social and economic characteristics of African-American scholars who pursued graduate study through the Lilly program. Educational and employment histories are also analyzed. Perhaps of greatest significance, however, are the stories the scholars tell of their personal adaptations to the campus communities of their doctoral institutions. Such learning environments, in most cases, were large, predominantly white research institutions. The vital role of mentors or sponsors in the academic, social, and emotional adaptations of black graduate scholars is examined. These campus experiences and the extent to which they contributed to or weakened the scholar's chances of graduating must be considered in strategies designed to increase the number of blacks and other minorities who obtain doctoral degrees.

METHODOLOGY

To obtain our data, we surveyed a 100% sample of all faculty scholars in the Lilly program and presidents (or their representatives) of

United Negro College Fund institutions. Administrative records in the New York City office of the United Negro College Fund were examined; such records were those of successful faculty applicants awarded fellowships (see Appendix A for the application form), UNCF reports to the Lilly Endowment, and relevant correspondence between the Endowment and the Fund. Finally, information was gleaned from conferences and interviews. Conferences were held with presidents of UNCF member institutions and an advisory committee of five: two UNCF-college presidents, a former president of a UNCF institution who also was a former federal government administrator, and two senior administrators of the United Negro College Fund. Unstructured and semi-structured interviews were conducted with selected presidents of UNCF institutions at the June 1985, UNCF meeting in Virginia.

At this meeting, the purpose and methods of the evaluation study were explained and institutional cooperation was solicited by the principal investigator and the chief executive officer of the United Negro College Fund. Our questionnaire (see Appendix B) was distributed to UNCF-college presidents at this session. As a result of follow-up telephone calls, and a series of mailgrams, 31 of the presidents (72%) completed the questionnaire. They provided information about their recruitment procedures for faculty scholars who received graduate study grants and gave an assessment of the value of this faculty development program for the educational mission of their institutions.

Names of faculty members awarded fellowships, the year in which the fellowships were awarded, and information on whether faculty scholars had completed study for the doctoral degree were obtained from files of the United Negro College Fund. Faculty scholars were surveyed by mail. An 11-page questionnaire requested personal data such as age, sex, race, marital status, and number of dependents (see Appendix C). Family background data were obtained, including the educational and occupational attainment of parents and siblings as well as the occupational and educational history of the fellowship recipients. Detailed information on graduate study was requested, including the name of institutions attended for baccalaureate and graduate degrees, the region of institutions of baccalaureate and graduate study, graduate fields of specialization, and experiences with administrators, faculty, and students in schools of graduate study. Finally, faculty scholars were asked to indicate what impact, if any, graduate study had on their careers. The questionnaire also elicited opinions from scholars on whether they could have continued their graduate study without fellowship assistance, and what changes, if any, they would recommend to make the UNCF/ Lilly Faculty Development Program more effective.

United Negro College Fund records indicate that 146 faculty members received fellowships between 1977 and 1984. Questionnaires were sent to 143 faculty scholars for whom addresses were known. Thus, the size of the study population cited varies by three depending on whether the UNCF or the survey data are used.

Of the 143 faculty scholars surveyed, some received questionnaires and did not respond, and 25 questionnaires were returned undeliverable to the scholars. The 65 who responded by completing questionnaires represented 46% of the 143 scholars. If the 25 returned questionnaires that could not be delivered because of death or the absence of a forwarding address are subtracted from 143, the response rate increases to 55% of 118 scholars contacted.

One indication that the sample of 65 faculty scholars who completed the questionnaire may be similar to the fellowship recipients with a known address who did not is the percentage that completed graduate study in the two groups: According to the UNCF records, 28% of the total population of 146 faculty scholars completed doctorates, as did 31% of the 65 faculty scholars who returned the questionnaire.

Three waves of mailings were sent to faculty scholars. Memorandums from the principal investigator and from an officer of the Lilly Endowment were included in one mailing. Their messages indicated the effects the responses of scholars might have on future funding decisions and urged participation in the survey as a way for scholars to tell their own story. Later mailings included a plea from the principal investigator for cooperation and a memorandum from an officer of the United Negro College Fund. The fact that some members of the evaluation study team were black and had direct experience in UNCF institutions was emphasized.

A problem in collecting data by way of a mailed survey was the absence of permanent addresses of fellowship recipients. Letters to faculty scholars, therefore, were addressed to them at the institutions where they were employed when the fellowship was awarded. Some had left these institutions. That many in the fellowship population had moved and could not be reached by mail is reflective of the high rate of geographical mobility found among some professionals in the early stages of a career.

The total population of faculty scholars studied was affiliated with 37 UNCF institutions. Six UNCF institutions had not participated in the fellowship program during the eight-year period of investigation. Thus, the program served 86% of the private black colleges and universities that are members of the United Negro College Fund.

REVIEW OF RESEARCH

The Lilly/UNCF Faculty Development Program has served a dual purpose of providing an opportunity for young black faculty to become fully credentialed scholars and of enhancing the status of the private black colleges as learning environments. These institutions are where most African-Americans obtained a college education during the first half of the twentieth century and earlier.

Fleming (1984) reports that the "mass entrance" of black students onto white campuses occurred in the 1960s. By the mid-1970s, two-thirds to three-fourths of blacks were attending predominantly white institutions (Boyd, 1974; Gurin & Epps, 1975). However, the momentum of increased black enrollment in higher education that grew during the late 1960s and early 1970s has since waned.

Gail Thomas' (1987) study of the status of black students in U.S. graduate and professional schools corroborates the findings of antecedent works in this area. Thomas' analysis alerts us to the diminishing proportion of African-Americans in graduate and professional schools relative to their availability in the baccalaureate pool. Blacks in the natural and technical sciences are significantly underrepresented. Thomas (1981) concludes that both individual and institutional responses are needed to promote greater minority enrollment and retention.

Alexander Astin's (1982) study of persistence among black graduate and professional students had as one premise that "higher education serves as a principal gatekeeper for entry into the most prestigious and lucrative careers" (p. 1). Astin found that dropout rates among minority students at each "transitional point" in the higher education pipeline, including graduate and professional schools, are "substantially higher than those for whites" (p. 2). These rates were most pronounced for Hispanics and Native Americans. Astin concluded that these "leakage points" predict a future worsening of the "grossly underrepresented" status of blacks and other minorities in academic and professional circles (p. 25).

Fleming (1984) found that predominantly white institutions tend to minimize the magnitude of adjustment required of African-Americans who move from all-black to the mostly all-white settings. Most of the scholars in our study attended historically black colleges as undergraduates and predominantly white institutions for graduate study. Fleming cites Leovinger's "supportive community" criteria in discussing the interpersonal needs of black students on the predominantly white campus, noting that "supportive interpersonal relations are not only desirable but necessary for development during college years" (p. 151). Further, opportunities for friendships, participation in the life of the campus, and a sense of progress and success in their academic pursuits are critical for the well-being of all students, including black graduate students.

Some scholars have attempted to explore the issue of attrition and persistence of minority graduate students by examining the attitudinal and interpersonal dynamics of the campus experience of these students. Because of a dearth of empirical studies in the area of minority experiences at the graduate level, much about this phenomenon must be inferred from the experiences of undergraduates. In Charles Willie's and Arline McCord's (1972) analysis of black undergraduates at four postsecondary predominantly white institutions, black students reported that they expected "less prejudice and more social integration than they actually experienced in their predominantly white colleges" (p. 104).

In exploring the performances of African-Americans at such schools, Michael Nettles (1988) concluded that "efforts to improve [their] college grade-point averages should focus upon improving their relationships with faculty and should also address their relative dissatisfaction with academic environment" (p. 27). According to Nettles, "black students have significantly less contact with faculty outside the classroom than white students and this contributes to the lower grades for black students" (p. 29).

Walter Allen (1986) provides an analysis of the experiences of black students on predominantly white campuses with their teachers. While two out of every three black students report "good" relationships, only one-sixth have "excellent" relationships with teachers; this positive proportion is offset by one-sixth that have "poor" relationships with teachers.

Yvonne Abatso (1987) discovered that both institutional and personal characteristics influence a student's ability to cope with a school. On the institutional side, higher retention rates were prevalent at schools with strong administrative support systems that emphasize academic growth and development. Those students with a greater sense of control over their destiny tended to persist through the full matriculation cycle; such students were better able than other students to find sources of financial support. Financial support, of course, is a key ingredient in persistence.

Willie and McCord (1972) also found that some black students tended to distrust predominantly white universities. The source of this distrust was sometimes an isolated incident involving an instructor's evaluation that a student felt was unfair or the unsatisfactory resolution of a dispute with the university. Because of these feelings, some black students tried to seek out a black authority figure as "an intercessor" to negotiate with the university on their behalf. Willie and Donald Cunnigen (1981) revisit Alexander Leighton's (1946) three basic human adaptations to "emotional disturbances" in examining the plight of black students frustrated with an all-white setting. They observed that flexible use of "cooperation, withdrawal and aggressiveness . . . is [useful for] blacks who make an effective adaptation to predominantly white college campuses" (p. 193).

These authors also indicated the need of a support system for African-Americans enrolled in a predominantly white setting. If the first year of graduate study generates the greatest stress (Gibbs, 1974), the absence of adequate support services could affect the willingness of black students to persevere through upper division and graduate study, which are academically more demanding.

Blackwell (1987) has observed that a "poor fit" exists between the values, perceptions, and demographic characteristics of black graduate school candidates and admissions officers. His study found that university officials tended to evaluate more favorably the candidates from traditionally white institutions than graduates of predominantly black colleges and universities even though the black applicants may have had comparable records.

Astin (1982) cites research on the impact of the *Bakke* and *Defunis* United States Supreme Court cases (O'Neil, 1975; Tollett, 1978). This research helps to explain the climate of growing resistance in the higher education community to affirmative action and special admissions programs for minority students. There is the belief that colleges and universities "have gone too far in accommodating the special needs of minority students" (Astin, 1982, p. 5). Despite the need for renewed efforts in the recruitment and retention of African-American students at all levels of higher education, Astin detects the presence of subtle hostility by some higher education authorities that may be associated with outcomes of these court cases.

William Trent and Elaine Copeland (1988) explored reasons for the "precipitous decrease" in black graduate students between 1972 and 1984. In their case study of five Title VI states, these authors discovered inconsistent efforts to recruit and retain black doctoral candidates. While most states were strong on recruitment of African-Americans by providing adequate first-year support, they were weaker on retention. Trent and Copeland concluded that there is greater pressure for parity than retention. The decrease in black graduate students noted by Trent and Copeland has been confirmed by national statistics that show a 20% drop in the number of black graduate students between 1976 and 1982, from 22,058 to 17,883 (Thomas, 1987).

The college completion rate of African-Americans almost doubled between 1970 and 1980. Blackwell (1987) attributes this to a number of factors, including "increased federal financial aid" (p. 71). Blackwell observed that as the federal support for higher education declined during the Reagan administration, colleges and universities did not pick up the slack for black graduate students. He found, for example, that "whites are more likely to be awarded fellowships and graduate teaching assistantships than are black students" (p. 73). Blackwell believes that these combinations of practices and other events, such as the *Bakke* decision, stalled the rate of increase of blacks in graduate and professional schools. In summary, he found that "black students are more likely to be enrolled in those [graduate and professional] institutions with favorable financial assistance programs for them" and that "black students [are] more likely to enroll in professional schools if they operate a special admissions program" (pp. 86–87).

Studying the policy process surrounding the implementation of criteria required in the *Adams* case filed in 1970 against segregated higher education in public colleges, James Upton and Anne Pruitt (1985) concluded that "financial aid dispensed should be separated into targeted and non-targeted aid . . . [including] aid targeted specifically for black graduate students" (p. 95). They report that it is important to do this because they "expect that racial differences in financial aid distribution will affect the number of black students who receive Ph.D.s" (p. 95).

Gloria Scott (1981) has reported that "the majority of black students come from families with inadequate socioeconomic resources" (p. 358). These students need financial aid not only for tuition but also for room and board and books. Scott said the absence of funds to cover these costs is as important as "or more important than the tuition costs in preventing college attendance" (p. 359). According to Scott, the G.I. Bill enacted in 1944 was very effective in opening higher education opportunities to minorities because it "provided students with subsistence and the cost of books and tuition" (p. 359). This is needed, in her opinion, because "black students, both graduate and undergraduate, are excluded from access to full participation in federal contracts and grants awarded to predominantly white institutions" (pp. 364, 368). Exclusion from the graduate assistantships associated with federal grants to research universities impeded the academic development of African-American students. Scott observes that such support would enhance the probability of more blacks achieving a college or university education.

In the light of these findings and others, the Commission on the Higher Education of Minorities has called for an "increase [in] the amount of financial aid available for minority graduate students as well as . . . strengthen[ed] institutional commitment to the goal of increasing minority enrollments" (Astin, 1982, p. 201). There is a connection between increased minority presence in higher education and increased financial aid. In addition, the Commission has recommended that "every effort should be made to expand the number of assistantships available to minority graduate students, since this form of aid seems to intensify student involvement in graduate study, promote professional development, and strengthen the bond between student and faculty mentor" (p. 201).

The Commission appropriately mentioned faculty mentors. They are essential in graduate education and career development. Daniel Levinson (1978) noted that it is extremely difficult for women and minorities to find mentors. Willie (1987) states that "mentors not only teach and advise, they also sponsor. Mentors believe in their proteges. They share their [own] dreams and experience with . . . [their proteges, as well as sharing the proteges'] pain and disappointments" (p. 99).

Based on a national study of 157 black professionals, Blackwell (1983) found that "only about 12.2% of the respondents had mentors" (p. 95). This finding caused Blackwell to concur with Levinson and conclude that "true mentors are difficult to acquire for black students" (p. 97). The importance of mentors is discussed in Chapter 7.

Our discussion in the rest of this book is focused on how background and campus experiences negatively or positively affect the retention rate of black graduate students. The findings were derived from the survey of UNCF faculty scholars who received Lilly Endowment grants for doctoral study. The extent to which the analysis of these data confirms or casts doubt on findings cited in the literature review will be noted.

4 Analysis of Program Outcomes

This chapter examines the association between degree-completion status and length of time of graduate study. Antecedent variables such as undergraduate performance and grade-point average during the course of graduate studies are analyzed. Also examined are family characteristics such as number of dependents and the educational achievement of spouse and parents of scholars to determine their association, if any, with degree-completion status. Finally, family financial circumstances are studied, including the amount and number of grants and awards received in support of graduate study and how these affect degree-completion status.

DEGREE STATUS OF FACULTY SCHOLARS

Because the Lilly/UNCF Faculty Development Program was established to increase the representation of faculty with doctoral degrees at UNCF institutions, we first want to examine the doctoral program completion rate of the 65 faculty scholars who responded to our questionnaire. The program status of all participants in this study is represented in Table 4.1. The range extended from those scholars in the initial stage of taking required courses to those in the final stage of writing a thesis. Scholars are classified according to the stage of completion in their program of study at the time they submitted the questionnaire.

If the several stages of a doctoral program are collapsed into three—the course work stage, the writing stage, and the degree-completion stage—we find that 26% of the faculty scholars in our sample were either taking or had just finished taking courses, and had not yet begun the thesis-writing stage. The largest proportion of faculty scholars (39%) were writing a required pre-thesis qualifying paper or the thesis itself. Thirty-two percent of the respondents had received degrees, most of this number returning to their full-time teaching positions at a UNCF institution. The remaining 3% had

TABLE 4.1 Doctoral Program Status of Faculty Scholars

Program Status	n	%
Taking Courses	7	10.8
Completed Courses	10	15.4
Completed Qualifying Paper	5	7.7
Writing Thesis	20	30.8
Completed Thesis	2	3.1
Received Doctorate	21	32.3
Total	65	100.0

completed all requirements for the doctoral degree and were awaiting graduation ceremonies.

One may consider the doctoral study of faculty scholars by tracking them from the first year of Lilly fellowship assistance (see Table 4.2). The longer scholars have been enrolled in a doctoral program, the greater is the probability that they will have completed degree requirements. We have grouped the first-year grant classes into four 2-year cohorts. The first cohort included the years 1977–78, and the last, 1983–84. The faculty scholars who responded to the questionnaire tended to be those who had received grants after 1981; thus half of the 8-year study period was underrepresented in the sample, while those who received grants in 1983–84 are overrepresented. Forty-five percent of the respondents first received a Lilly faculty development grant during this period. The number of scholars in each of the cohort periods ranges from 7 to 29. Proportions based on such small numbers are not as reliable indicators as one might wish; thus, caution is advised in the interpretation of these findings. The important fact to consider, however, is the distribution pattern of proportions in the four-cohort series.

Table 4.2 presents several interesting trends among faculty scholars with respect to degree-completion. Working forward from the earliest years of fellowship activity, we found that 58% of the 1977–78 cohort of grant recipients had completed degrees. For the 1979–80 cohort, the degree-completion rate decreased to 43%; for the 1981–82 cohort, it was 41%. There was a degree-completion rate of 14% for scholars who received grants after 1983. All scholars with terminal degrees in this most recent cohort received Lilly grants in 1983. Clearly a 2-year period of fellowship support is too short to obtain maximum benefit from a program in which the goal is degree-com-

TABLE 4.2 Degree-Completion Status of Faculty Scholars

Grant Year	Doctorate		No Doctorate		Total	
	n	%	n	%	n	%
1977-78	7	33.3	5	11.4	12	18.5
1979-80	3	14.3	4	9.1	7	10.8
1981-82	7	33.3	10	22.7	17	26.2
1983-84	4	19.0	25	56.8	29	44.6
Total	21	100.0	44	100.0	65	100.0

pletion. The proportion of scholars who receive doctoral degrees after studying 6 years compared with those who have studied only 2 years increases by a factor of four. Indeed, more than 6 years of study is required before a majority of the scholars in any of the cohorts were awarded terminal degrees. This finding has implications for policies pertaining to the number of years that a grant for doctoral study will be offered or renewed.

ACADEMIC RECORD OF SCHOLARS

Faculty scholars were asked to give self-reports of their undergraduate and doctoral academic records. For the sake of uniformity, college and graduate grades were converted to a standard 4-point grade scale. Table 4.3 indicates that a majority of the faculty scholars maintained "B—" to "B" averages as undergraduates. While some in the study sample earned higher and lower grade-point averages, achievement as undergraduates seemed to be unrelated to whether a grant recipient had completed his or her doctoral degree. A variation of only a few percentage points exists among scholars who had "A" or "B" grade-point averages as undergraduates and who had or had not completed their doctoral degrees. Undergraduates' educational achievement was similar for graduate scholars in both degree-completion categories.

About 63% of the sample of faculty scholars had an "A," an "A—," or a "B+" average in their graduate academic records; and 37% had an average of "B" or "B—." Faculty scholars who had completed degree requirements tended to be more frequently represented in the B+ and above category for graduate studies. Four out of 10 scholars with a grade-point average of B+ or better are found in

TABLE 4.3 Academic Performance of Faculty Scholars

Grade-Point Average	Doctorate		No Doctorate		Total	
	n	%	n	%	n	%
Undergraduate						
3.70 and Above	8	38.1	15	34.9	23	35.9
(B+, A-, A)						
2.75-3.69	11	52.4	22	51.2	33	51.6
(B-, B)						
1.75-2.74	2	9.5	6	14.0	8	12.5
(C-, C, C+)						
Below 1.70	0	0.0	0	0.0	0	0.0
Total	21	100.0	43	100.0	64	100.0
Doctoral						
3.70 and Above	16	76.2	24	57.1	40	63.5
(B+, A-, A)						
2.75-3.69	5	23.8	18	42.9	23	36.5
(B-, B)						
1.75-2.74	0	0.0	0	0.0	0	0.0
(C-, C, C+)						
Below 1.70	0	0.0	0	0.0	0	0.0
Total	21	100.0	42	100.0	63	100.0

the "doctorate" category, but only about 2 of 10 with a grade-point average of B or B— had earned a degree. These facts mean that nearly 8 of 10 scholars with grade-point averages of B or B— for graduate studies had not earned a doctorate when this report was prepared, but only 6 of 10 with grade-point averages of B+ and above were still studying for the terminal degree. These findings suggest that scholars who successfully complete requirements for the doctorate do so with stronger graduate school academic records than scholars who do not complete their degrees in a timely fashion.

PERSONAL AND FAMILY BACKGROUND VARIABLES

Table 4.4 presents a summary of information on the demographic characteristics of the study population. The average scholar is 42 years of age; the oldest in this sample is 58 and the youngest, 28.

TABLE 4.4 Demographic Characteristics of Faculty Scholars

Characteristics	n	%
Sex of Faculty		
Female	38	58.5
Male	27	41.5
Total	65	100.0
Race of Faculty		
Black	56	86.2
White	8	12.3
Other	1	1.5
Total	65	100.0
Family Status		
Single	12	18.5
Divorced	9	13.8
Separated	1	1.5
Married	43	66.2
Total	65	100.0
Rank Among Siblings		
Only Child	6	9.5
Youngest Child	15	23.8
Middle Child	23	36.5
Oldest Child	19	30.2
Total	63	100.0
Age of Faculty	64	42.4 years
Offspring	64	1.5 children

Women awarded fellowships outnumber men 59% to 41%. The group is racially diversified but predominantly black; 86% are black, 12% white, and 2% other. Most of these scholars are southern-born and grew up in small towns or rural communities.

Two-thirds of the faculty scholars are married, and 19% are single; the remainder (15%) are separated or divorced, as seen in Table 4.4. In this predominantly black population of college graduates, the number of offspring in families formed through marriage ranges from none to four, averaging between one and two children per household.

With the data in Table 4.5, we can explore the link between selected personal and family background characteristics of the faculty

TABLE 4.5 Personal and Family Background Characteristics

Characteristics	Doctorate n	Doctorate %	No Doctorate n	No Doctorate %	Total n	Total %
Sex						
Male	11	52.4	16	36.4	27	41.5
Female	10	47.6	28	63.6	38	58.5
Total	21	100.0	44	100.0	65	100.0
Number of Dependents						
0	4	20.0	11	25.0	15	23.4
1-2	16	80.0	27	61.4	43	67.2
3-4	0	0.0	6	13.6	6	9.4
Total	20	100.0	44	100.0	64	100.0
Family Status						
Married	15	71.4	23	63.9	38	66.7
Single	3	14.3	6	16.7	9	15.8
Divorced	3	14.3	6	16.7	9	15.8
Separated	0	0.0	1	2.8	1	1.8
Total	21	100.0	36	100.0	57	100.0

scholars and the completion of doctoral studies. Table 4.5 displays gender, number of dependents, and family status data according to doctoral status (with degree/without degree) of the responding scholars. As pointed out, 59% of the total sample of 65 respondents are female. But males are overrepresented in the degree-holder category by approximately 15 percentage points, a finding that requires additional study to determine if a significant relationship exists between gender and degree status.

The data on number of household dependents show that two-thirds of the scholars have either one or two dependents at home. Specifically, there are, on average, 1.4 dependents per household. Although a majority of the faculty scholars are married, several are childless couples or the parents of only one child. A small number of faculty scholars—6 of 64—have three to four dependents. None of this small group with the largest number of dependents had completed the doctoral degree. Nevertheless, we conclude that family size is of limited value as a predictor of degree-completion status. While large households with several dependents tend to be associated with the "no doctorate" category more frequently than with the "doctorate" category, very few of the households are large.

Table 4.6 represents the level of formal education attained by the scholars' three closest adult relatives: mother, father, and spouse. The most striking feature of this analysis is the rich educational background of their spouses. Sixty-five percent of the husbands and wives in the households of scholars studying for a doctorate are currently enrolled or have been enrolled in graduate school; 80% of the spouses graduated from college. Presumably, a scholar's high regard for

TABLE 4.6 Educational Attainment of Adult Relatives of Faculty Scholars

Educational Attainment	Doctorate n	Doctorate %	No Doctorate n	No Doctorate %	Total n	Total %
Spouse						
Grade School	0	0.0	0	0.0	0	0.0
Some High School	0	0.0	0	0.0	0	0.0
High School Grad	1	6.3	2	6.7	3	6.5
Some College	1	6.3	5	16.7	6	13.0
College Grad	1	6.3	6	20.0	7	15.2
Graduate School	13	81.3	17	56.7	30	65.2
Total	16	100.0	30	100.0	46	100.0
Mother						
Grade School	10	47.6	14	32.6	24	37.5
Some High School	0	0.0	6	14.0	6	9.4
High School Grad	4	19.0	9	20.9	13	20.3
Some College	5	23.8	8	18.6	13	20.3
College Grad	0	0.0	1	2.3	1	1.6
Graduate School	2	9.5	5	11.6	7	10.9
Total	21	100.0	43	100.0	64	100.0
Father						
Grade School	6	30.0	15	35.7	21	33.9
Some High School	4	20.0	8	19.0	12	19.4
High School Grad	3	15.0	10	23.8	13	21.0
Some College	1	5.0	4	9.5	5	8.1
College Grad	3	15.0	1	2.4	4	6.5
Graduate School	3	15.0	4	9.5	7	11.3
Total	20	100.0	42	100.0	62	100.0

higher education, including graduate education, is reinforced, if not inspired, by a highly educated spouse. The fact that both spouses have experienced graduate study in most households in this study also has financial implications for the debt that families may be shouldering.

When a comparison is made of the education of spouses of scholars who had received a doctoral degree with the education of spouses of those who had not, spouses of husbands or wives who had earned their degrees tended to be found more frequently in the category of spouses with graduate degrees than the spouses of husbands or wives who had not completed their studies. We also note that scholars who had not completed their degrees were more frequently married to persons who had not yet finished college than scholars who had completed their graduate studies.

Findings pertaining to the educational history of the parents of the faculty scholars are intriguing, too. Only one-sixth of the parents of these African-American scholars pursuing doctoral studies had graduated from college. It should be noted that both mothers and fathers of these scholars had attained more or less similar levels of formal schooling. The educational attainment of the scholars compared with that of both parents represented a generational leap forward. A majority of the parents had only a high school education or less. Graduate school study had been experienced by only one-tenth of the parents of these scholars who were studying for doctoral degrees. More research is needed on why offspring are motivated to pursue graduate education in families in which parents have not attended college.

In the early 1960s, James Morgan and Associates (1962) of the University of Michigan studied income and welfare experiences in the United States and concluded:

> An average education attained by children is . . . influenced by the educational achievement of the mother. The more education the wife has relative to the husband, the more education the children attain. . . . Where the wife has less education than [her husband], achievement of the children is impeded but not so much as . . . [their achievement is] advanced when the wife has more education than her husband. (pp. 374–375)

This study of African-Americans with high levels of educational attainment has findings that are similar to the University of Michigan study. Despite the apparent similarity in educational achievement of both parents, closer inspection reveals that 33% of the mothers in this study (compared with 26% of the fathers) had attended college. Also, slightly fewer mothers compared with fathers failed to graduate from high school. Thus, the mothers had as much, and in some instances a little more, education than the fathers. These data and their analysis do indeed suggest that the educational attainment of offspring is enhanced when the mother in a family has as much education as the father. This finding has great implications regarding the value of providing higher education for women and the effects of this practice on future generations.

FINANCIAL SUPPORT SYSTEM DURING STUDY

A crucial determinant in the successful completion of a graduate degree program is the presence of an adequate source of financial assistance. This section examines the extent to which scholars must work in order to meet living expenses while studying and what, if any, financial support UNCF schools are able to provide to faculty on study-leave. Tables 4.7 and 4.8 portray three dimensions of this issue: the proportion of scholars required to work, their weekly workload in average number of hours, and the form of support provided by their employers, the UNCF institutions.

From data presented in Table 4.7 we can see that approximately half of the faculty scholars in graduate school had to work to provide additional income for living expenses not covered by their grants or other financial aid. Table 4.8 shows a wide range of weekly schedules for the working scholars. One-fourth were able to get by with less than 10 hours of outside work per week; one-third worked between 11 and 20 hours; 40% of the scholars, however, had to work over 20 hours a week.

As shown in Table 4.9, the 65 faculty scholars in this study

TABLE 4.7 Need to Work While in Doctoral Program

	Doctorate		No Doctorate		Total	
	n	**%**	**n**	**%**	**n**	**%**
Need to Work	11	52.4	22	51.2	33	51.6
No Need to Work	10	47.6	21	48.8	31	48.4
Total	21	100.0	43	100.0	64	100.0

received an average award slightly in excess of $29,000 from all sources of support. Since the average length of study was approximately 4 years, each faculty scholar received an average annual grant of about $7,500. This dollar figure represents the actual amount of

TABLE 4.8   Financial Support System of Faculty Scholars

	n	%
Hours per Week (for Workers)		
1-10	8	26.7
11-20	10	33.3
21-30	7	23.3
Over 30	5	16.7
Total	30	100.0
Form of UNCF Support		
None	27	45.0
Fringe Benefits	6	10.0
Partial Salary	16	26.7
Full Salary	11	18.3
Total	60	100.0

TABLE 4.9   Financial Circumstances of Faculty Scholars

Average total financial assistance package per scholar from all sources (n=56)	$29,173
Average number of years of assistance from all sources (n=65)	3.89 years
Average total number of grants per scholar from all sources (n=56)	3.4 grants
Average total support of scholar by Lilly Endowment (n=63)	$18,029
Percentage of total financial support of scholars by Lilly Endowment (n=55)	72.9%
Average number of Lilly grants per scholar	1.7 grants

money awarded up to 1985. It has not been converted into constant dollars.

The scholars received an average of three to four grants (3.4) to assist them in their studies; one or more of these were Lilly grants. Lilly grants were renewable, although only a minority of the faculty scholars received multiple grants from this source. Table 4.9 shows that overall this group of scholars received an average of 1.7 grants from Lilly during the course of their graduate study. The one or two grants from the Lilly Endowment averaged just over $18,000 and accounted for about 73% of the total financial support of the faculty scholars.

Grants from other sources were required because most faculty scholars had not completed more than 3 years of graduate study when the final Lilly grant was awarded, as seen in Table 4.10. While a majority of the scholars required 4 or more years to complete work for their degrees, only 32% received a Lilly grant after the fourth year of matriculation. At least 40% of the scholars received their only or last Lilly grant in their first or second year of graduate study. Even with help from other sources, two-thirds of the scholars (63%) did not have any grant support from Lilly or elsewhere after the fourth year of graduate study.

Those scholars not supported beyond the second year of gradu-ate study may be expected to encounter difficulty in fulfilling doctoral degree requirements. Our data revealed that three-fourths of the faculty scholars who had been admitted to the Lilly program between

TABLE 4.10 Year in Doctoral Study by First and Last Lilly Grant and Last Grant from Any Source

Year in Doctoral Program	First Lilly		Last Lilly		Last Grant	
	n	**%**	**n**	**%**	**n**	**%**
First Year	20	40.8	6	9.2	4	6.2
Second Year	15	30.6	20	30.8	15	23.1
Third Year	3	6.1	12	18.5	15	23.1
Fourth Year	3	6.1	6	9.2	7	10.8
Fifth Year	4	8.2	6	9.2	10	15.4
Sixth Year and Beyond	4	8.2	15	23.1	14	21.5
Total	49	100.0	65	100.0	65	100.0

1977 and 1984 and who had received doctorates at the end of the 1984 school year were candidates 3 to 7 years before their degrees were awarded. These findings suggest that a cutoff period of 2 years may be too soon. As stated earlier, most scholars had not completed more than 3 years of graduate study when the last Lilly grant was received; many had only 4 years of graduate study when the last grant from any source was received. In these circumstances, a substantial number of faculty scholars in United Negro College Fund institutions were left without any form of assistance, except personal resources derived from employment while pursuing a graduate degree.

The resources of UNCF institutions are scarce. Few can do more than offer a leave of absence without pay for faculty to pursue full-time graduate study (refer to Table 4.8). About one-half of the colleges provided no financial assistance beyond, perhaps, payment of fringe benefits while a faculty member was on leave. Less than one-fifth was able to continue a faculty member's full salary while he or she was on leave. Resources at graduate schools of matriculation are not readily available to UNCF faculty scholars either. A majority of these African-American scholars had little, if any, opportunity to serve as research or teaching assistants.

Thus, many scholars were forced to work after their final grant-in-aid for graduate study was awarded. The average number of hours that faculty scholars worked while studying is 11 to 12 hours per week. A few worked full time. Such long hours of work, of course, further cut into study time and can delay degree completion beyond the usual amount of time required.

CONCLUSIONS

The scholars who had received fellowships and who had earned doctoral degrees during the study period had undergraduate academic records that were similar to those who had not yet earned their doctoral degrees. Failure to complete graduate studies in a timely fashion seemed to be a function of experience other than undergraduate academic performance.

All graduate students were performing well. Nearly two-thirds had B+ or better grade-point averages. However, those who had completed their work in a timely fashion tended to have better grades in graduate school than those who required more time. Since both groups had similar undergraduate records, the experiences that delayed completion of graduate work probably were contemporaneous with graduate study and not antecedent to it. The same factors that probably delayed progress toward degree-completion also could have interfered with the quality of graduate work performed. Indeed the data revealed that a higher proportion of scholars with relatively large families and labor force participants of more than 20 hours per week were among those still pursuing graduate studies.

These findings have implications for grant-making policy. A majority of the scholars required more than 5 years to obtain their degrees. Yet most received their final grants the fourth year of study or earlier. In addition, these students had fewer opportunities to be teaching and research assistants in their schools of matriculation after grants had expired.

By not making funds available to African-American scholars beyond the fourth year of graduate study, granting agencies place such students and their investments in them at risk. Data from this study suggest that some students may never complete their degrees because of the combined pressures of increased family responsibilities and diminished financial assistance. The most appropriate length of funding period for black graduate students is an issue in need of much study. On the basis of these findings, periods of support longer than 4 years may be necessary to ensure successful degree-completion.

5 Education and Employment of Faculty Scholars

This chapter presents data on the employment and educational experiences of scholars in this study. Information is analyzed about the location of universities in which programs of graduate study were pursued, the scholars' fields of concentration, and their graduate and undergraduate records. The occupations of scholars and their levels of job responsibility before and after doctoral study are traced. Finally, retention rates for these newly credentialed scholars as professional educators and as faculty and staff of United Negro College Fund institutions are analyzed.

EMPLOYMENT

The sample of 65 scholars were employed by 28 of the 43 United Negro College Fund institutions. As indicated in Table 5.1, most colleges had only one to three faculty members with fellowship appointments during the 8-year study period, although two colleges captured as many as six appointments during these years. Together, the scholars averaged 10 years of employment in United Negro College Fund institutions. Some had worked in these colleges as many as 26 years and others as few as 3 years. In addition to working in black colleges, 7 to 8 out of every 10 had received a bachelor's degree from a private or public black college, according to data in Table 5.2. Most of the predominantly black institutions that these faculty scholars attended as undergraduates were United Negro College Fund institutions. Yet, as a group, their education and employment affiliations are not exclusively limited to their *alma mater*; only about 1 in 4 is employed in the same college from which a baccalaureate degree was earned.

41

TABLE 5.1   Number of Faculty Scholars per Individual College, 1977-84

Scholars per College	Colleges	
	n	%
One	13	46.4
Two	2	7.1
Three	9	32.1
Four	1	3.6
Five	1	3.6
Six	2	7.1
Total	28	100.0

TABLE 5.2   Racial Composition of Institutions Attended by Faculty Scholars

Level of Institution	Scholars	
	n	%
Undergraduate		
Predominantly white	17	27.4
Predominantly black	45	72.6
Total	62	100.0
Doctoral		
Predominantly white	57	90.5
Predominantly black	6	9.5
Total	63	100.0

LOCATION OF DOCTORAL PROGRAMS

The faculty scholars attended 42 different universities to pursue studies for their doctoral degrees. These universities were scattered throughout the nation in 18 of the 50 states and in the District of Columbia, as seen in Table 5.3. About 65% of graduate schools of matriculation are located in the South, including such states as Alabama, Florida, Georgia, Mississippi, North Carolina, South Carolina, Tennessee, Texas, and Virginia; the remainder are located elsewhere in all regions of the United States.

Georgia reigns supreme as the state of first choice for graduate study by a plurality of the faculty scholars in this study. The largest

TABLE 5.3 Location by State of Doctoral Institutions
Attended by Faculty Scholars

State	n	%
Alabama	2	3.2
Arizona	1	1.6
California	1	1.6
District of Columbia	5	8.1
Florida	2	3.2
Georgia	14	22.6
Iowa	1	1.6
Illinois	1	1.6
Indiana	2	3.2
Mississippi	3	4.8
North Carolina	4	6.5
New Jersey	2	3.2
New York	3	4.8
Ohio	5	8.1
South Carolina	4	6.5
Tennessee	3	4.9
Texas	6	9.7
Virginia	2	3.2
Wisconsin	1	1.2
Total	62	100.0

proportion enrolled in Emory University in Atlanta. It accommodated 13% of the doctoral students. When Emory is combined with
other Georgia-based institutions such as Georgia State University in
Atlanta, the University of Georgia in Athens, and Atlanta University,
23% of the faculty scholars pursued graduate studies in Georgia. The
second highest percentage of faculty scholars studied in universities in
Texas. However, this proportion is only about 10% compared with
Georgia's 23%. Georgia, of course, is the home state for more United
Negro College Fund institutions than any other state. Thus, some
faculty scholars tended to pursue graduate study near their home base
when possible, although some went to such distant states as Arizona,
California, Wisconsin, Illinois, Ohio, New York, and New Jersey. It is
appropriate to characterize the faculty scholars as both locally oriented and cosmopolitan in their selection of schools for graduate
study; more than half chose southern graduate schools, with less than
half choosing graduate schools outside the South.

FIELDS OF STUDY

Although faculty scholars pursued doctoral degrees in a number of different fields, as revealed in Table 5.4, they tended to cluster in three areas: humanities, 34%; education, 31%; and social sciences, 23%. Applied fields like business administration and social work accounted for about 6% of the scholars' concentrations. Science and mathematics combined were the fields of concentration for another 6 to 7%. If

TABLE 5.4 Academic Concentrations of Faculty Scholars in Bachelor's, Master's, and Doctoral Programs

Fields of Study	n	%
Doctoral		
Social Sciences	14	22.6
Education	19	30.6
Business Administration	3	4.8
Mathematics and Science	4	6.5
Humanities	21	33.9
Social Work	1	1.6
Other	0	0.0
Total	62	100.0
Master's		
Social Sciences	11	17.5
Education	11	17.5
Business Administration	5	7.9
Mathematics and Science	9	14.3
Humanities	23	36.5
Social Work	2	3.2
Other	2	3.2
Total	63	100.0
Bachelor's		
Social Sciences	11	18.3
Education	8	13.3
Business Administration	4	6.7
Mathematics and Science	8	13.3
Humanities	27	45.0
Social Work	0	0.0
Other	2	3.3
Total	60	100.0

the concentrations of the faculty scholars are grouped according to function, they reveal that slightly more than 6 of every 10 are interested in basic disciplines (organic and physical sciences, the social sciences, and humanities); and nearly 4 of every 10 are interested in fields that have to do with the application of knowledge such as education, business administration, and social work. These clusterings indicate some diversity among the faculty scholars in their academic interests; however, science and mathematics are generally underrepresented as fields of concentration.

That few faculty scholars pursued graduate degrees in science and mathematics does not mean that they did not have aptitudes for these fields. On the contrary, there is evidence from undergraduate records that the proportion (13%) enrolled in science and mathematics as major concentrations then was twice as great as the proportion enrolled in these fields for doctoral study. Indeed, interest in science and mathematics persisted through study for the master's degree; about 14% of the faculty scholars obtained a first-level graduate degree in these fields. Inexplicably, the shift of interest away from science and mathematics occurred with the commencement of doctoral degree studies.

ACADEMIC RECORD

As discussed in Chapter 4, the faculty scholars performed well as graduate students. Their overall average grade was B+, although some scholars had grade-point averages in the A range (refer to Table 4.3). None carried averages less than B— for graduate work. Undergraduate grade-point averages of faculty scholars ranged from C— to A—; as a group, their undergraduate average grade was B—. Thus, academic accomplishments in graduate study were definitely superior to those in undergraduate study.

A fact clearly established by an analysis of undergraduate and graduate academic records in Table 4.3 is that work performed for the baccalaureate degree is not always a good indicator of how well minority scholars will perform as graduate students. An indication of the motivation of some of these faculty scholars is the fact that they decided to seek a graduate degree in spite of less-than-excellent performances as undergraduates.

Among many African-American scholars, the achievement of a master's degree probably represents a milestone of greater import and a better indicator of academic promise than their undergraduate cumulative grade-point average. The desire to finally obtain a doctorate was manifested among 95% of the faculty scholars who had not yet attained this degree; this is a clear sign of the high aspirational level of individuals in this group. While 4 was the average number of years that faculty scholars had studied for the doctorate at the time of this investigation, at least one individual had pursued the dream of earning a doctorate for 14 years and had studied continually for this length of time. Many scholars required as many as 6 years of study. Motivation, perseverance, and endurance are appropriate descriptors of the academic character of these faculty scholars.

Apparently, the high motivation for the attainment of higher education was not unique to the scholars but was more or less a family phenomenon. Nine out of every 10 scholars in this study grew up in families that had two or more siblings. In most instances, the scholar had a brother or sister who was a college graduate too and worked in a professional occupation.

OCCUPATIONAL HISTORY

The intentions of the faculty scholars to obtain doctoral degrees are all the more remarkable in light of their occupational histories, as captured by data provided in Table 5.5. They were recruited into higher education from a number of jobs, some of which were outside the field of education. Forty-six percent worked in elementary and secondary school systems before employment in United Negro Col-

TABLE 5.5 Occupational History of Faculty Scholars

Area of Employment	n	%
Government Service	12	19.7
Elementary/Secondary Education	28	45.9
Business	3	4.9
Church/Social Service Agency	4	6.6
Homemaker	3	4.9
Higher Education	11	18.0
Total	61	100.0

lege Fund institutions; 26% (the next highest proportion) were employed in governmental or voluntary social service agencies. These agencies, together with the public schools, were the source of employment of nearly three-quarters (72.2%) of the scholars before they joined the faculty of a college or university. Actually, less than one-fifth (18%) of the scholars began their careers in higher education.

Table 5.6 provides data on the employment status of scholars immediately prior to their Lilly/UNCF grant experience. When faculty scholars initiated their studies for the doctoral degree, all were employed in a United Negro College Fund institution. Sixty-two percent held the rank of instructor or assistant professor. Less than 5% served as administrators.

POST-FELLOWSHIP EXPERIENCE

Table 5.7 shows that after completing doctoral studies, 9 out of every 10 scholars received promotions to the rank of associate professor or full professor or to an administrative position.

After pursuing a doctorate, as seen in Table 5.8, a few of the faculty scholars (8%) did not plan to return to UNCF schools. New employment usually was in business or a social service agency.

Although many scholars who completed study for a doctoral degree continued to work in UNCF schools, some sought employment elsewhere as soon as they were eligible (within the guidelines of the

TABLE 5.6 Faculty Rank of Scholars and Anticipated Career Advancement

Faculty Rank	Rank During Fellowship		Expected Rank After Fellowship	
	n	%	n	%
Instructor/Lecturer	7	11.5	2	9.1
Assistant Professor	31	50.8	1	4.5
Associate Professor	13	21.3	11	50.0
Professor	2	3.3	2	9.1
Department Chair	5	8.2	3	13.6
Administration	3	4.9	3	13.6
Total	61	100.0	22	100.0

TABLE 5.7 Employment Status of Faculty Scholars
After Earning Doctorate

Position	n	%
Vice President	1	4.8
Dean	2	9.5
Other Administrator	2	9.5
Division Head	2	9.5
Department Chair	1	4.8
Professor	5	23.8
Associate Professor	6	28.6
Non-Higher Education	2	9.5
Total	21	100.0

TABLE 5.8 Future Professional Plans of Faculty Scholars

Job Plans	Doctorate		No Doctorate		Total	
	n	%	n	%	n	%
Will return to UNCF school for 2 yrs	4	30.8	7	17.9	11	21.2
Will return to UNCF school for 5 yrs	2	15.4	8	20.5	10	19.2
Will return to UNCF school for at least 10 yrs	7	53.8	15	38.5	22	42.3
Will return to UNCF school, but prefers not	0	0.0	5	12.8	5	9.6
Will not return to UNCF school	0	0.0	4	10.3	4	7.7
Total	13	100.0	39	100.0	52	100.0

fellowship program, only 2 years of employment in a UNCF institution were required after receipt of a grant). Most of these individuals found work in a public school system or in a local governmental agency. We suspect that a substantial number of the faculty scholars who could not be reached because they had left the employment of their sponsoring college and had provided no forwarding address no longer work in higher education.

When asked about future plans, about 10% of the scholars indicated that they would return to a UNCF institution but would prefer not to return, 21% said that they planned to return to the sponsoring college for only the obligatory 2 years, and 19% anticipated returning for a maximum of 5 years (refer to Table 5.8). Together, these three categories account for one-half of the scholars who participated in this survey. This proportion, when added to the 8% who definitely did not plan to return to UNCF schools, means that in 5 years these institutions could lose over half of their teaching staff who received faculty development grants. These facts suggest that a faculty retention program, in addition to a faculty development program, is needed to enhance UNCF schools.

SUMMARY

Both locally oriented and cosmopolitan in their choice of graduate schools, more than half of the faculty scholars enrolled in southern schools, with less than half enrolled in graduate schools elsewhere in the nation. The average scholar concentrated in the humanities, education, or the social sciences. In general, this cohort of faculty scholars are good students; they are highly motivated, persevering individuals possessing records of solid academic achievement in their graduate studies.

The scholars manifested great loyalty to predominantly black colleges and universities. They work in such institutions, and most received bachelor's degrees from predominantly black colleges and universities. However, nearly half of the scholars who had completed degrees through this faculty development program could be recruited away from the campus of their sponsoring institutions in 5 or more years, if efforts are not undertaken to strengthen their commitment to their current employers.

6 Campus Experiences of Faculty Scholars

Some predominantly black colleges and universities now award the doctoral degree; however, the number of such schools is quite small. Of the scholars in this study, 90% matriculated at predominantly white institutions. As noted in Chapter 4, 86% of the scholars in this study are black, 12% white, and 2% other racial or ethnic minorities. This investigation, therefore, provides valuable information on what it is like to be an African-American scholar in an institution in which one is a member of a racial minority. It also indicates whether graduate study in a school with a student body that is similar to one's own racial population makes a difference in adaptation.

ADAPTATION OF BLACK SCHOLARS TO PREDOMINANTLY WHITE UNIVERSITIES

Helen Astin and Patricia Cross (1981) studied a sample of first-year black students enrolled in 393 institutions in 1976. Of those in predominantly white institutions, a majority said they attended such schools to get a better job (78.3% of men, 77.8% of women), thus enabling them to make more money (71% of men, 64.6% of women). Walter Allen (1981) studied 135 black students enrolled in the predominantly white University of North Carolina at Chapel Hill. He discovered findings similar to those reported above about employment aspirations among black collegians.

Allen also discovered some interesting findings about academic performance and student adaptations to the campus environment. Black students reported that feelings of alienation and anxiety negatively affect academic performance and that these feelings are greatly reduced when they "perceive that the University is committed to providing them with the necessary supportive services" (p. 136). Allen concluded that educational policy makers "must . . . begin to pay more attention to institutional processes" (p. 137). Indeed, he found that the more satisfied black students on predominantly white college campuses felt that campus race relations and the college's support were "positive."

A matrix of correlation coefficients for blacks derived from data gathered in the North Carolina study (Allen, 1981) revealed that the largest coefficient (.43) had to do with the association between the perceived race relations climate on campus and the relationships between students and professors. Those black students who had strong relationships with their professors also tended to feel that the campus race relations climate was positive. Black students who felt a positive race relations climate also tended to be more satisfied with their school of matriculation than did other black students. The correlation coefficient for the latter two variables was .35.

Opening predominantly white colleges and universities to African-American students and to other racial minorities is essential if the increasing numbers of such students who wish to pursue higher education are to be accommodated. But whether or not they will stay the course and become credentialed with a baccalaureate or graduate degree that will enhance their employment and income opportunities may depend a great deal on the campus experiences of these students. Alexander Astin (1982) reported that 72% of black students graduated from high school, but only 12% completed college and only 4% finished graduate or professional school. While the rising costs of higher education continue to present barriers for African-Americans and other racial minorities, the persistence of black students in institutions of higher education is, in part, a function of "the student's degree of involvement in campus life" (Cross & Astin, 1981, p. 84). Involvement in campus life clearly is related to social and psychological adaptations and whether black students at both graduate and undergraduate levels have the opportunity to meet new friends and interesting people. The social relationships that some black students experience on predominantly white college campuses cause them to feel that they are on trial (Willie, 1987). It is hard for people on trial to feel part of the community.

Our study of UNCF institutions and their faculty scholars who received Lilly Endowment grants to complete graduate study enabled us to determine whether the findings reported largely for undergraduate students in other studies also held for graduate students. Because a few faculty members of the UNCF colleges attended predominantly black graduate schools, this study was able to contrast the campus experiences of African-American students at predominantly black and at predominantly white graduate schools. Rodney Hartnett and

Benjamin Payton (1977) state that frequently the "reasons for [minorities] dropping out [of graduate school] are more personal or social than academic" (p. 8). While this particular analysis of the experience of UNCF faculty in pursuit of their doctoral degrees does not focus on dropout and retention rates of blacks, it does provide information on their academic, social, and psychological adaptations to various campus communities.

The questionnaire administered to the sample of participants in the fellowship program requested them to evaluate their social and academic experiences during graduate study. Faculty scholars were asked to indicate on a 4-point scale if they were (1) very dissatisfied, (2) dissatisfied, (3) satisfied, or (4) very satisfied with a wide group of campus experiences. Tables 6.1 and 6.2 group the responses of the 46 black scholars who attended predominantly white graduate schools and the six black scholars who attended predominantly black graduate schools. For the purpose of this analysis, the scholars were classified as satisfied if the average score for all who responded to the item was above 2.5; likewise, the scholars were characterized as dissatisfied if the average score for respondents was 2.5 or below.

Table 6.1 indicates that, with the exception of housing, black graduate students in this study who attended predominantly white graduate schools were satisfied with the physical environment and administrative services on campus. They were satisfied with (or had no complaints about) security, health services, food services, the library, and the recreational facilities. Also, they were satisfied with the quality of their educational experience. They were impressed with the competence of the administration and faculty and the quality of instruction.

The greatest areas of dissatisfaction for these black students at predominantly white graduate schools were the lack of opportunities to engage in collaborative work with faculty and the absence of racial diversity of the faculty. It could be that a more racially diversified faculty would have yielded more opportunities for African-Americans to collaborate with professors in professional work. This conjecture is strengthened by the finding that most black graduate students who had mentors chose individuals for that role who were affiliated with their racial population. The dissatisfaction by black graduate students with opportunities to engage in collaborative work with white faculty members in their predominantly white graduate schools includes dissatisfaction with opportunities to serve as teaching and research assistants.

Beyond dissatisfactions with these kinds of student–teacher inter-action, the blacks in this study were also dissatisfied with their social relationships on campus. They particularly mentioned the absence of friendliness among students; they were dissatisfied with the extent of their participation in student groups and in campus recreational activities. Because of these dissatisfactions, there is little wonder that most African-American graduate students, in general, were dis-pleased with the race relations climate on campus at predominantly white schools. They wanted more racial diversity in the student body and in the faculty.

ADAPTATION OF BLACK SCHOLARS
TO PREDOMINANTLY BLACK UNIVERSITIES

Black graduate students who attended predominantly black gradu-ate schools were few in number, only six. Their responses were tabulated in the same manner as responses of black students in predominantly white graduate schools. Table 6.2 displays the data for this analysis. Black students at predominantly black graduate schools tended to be dissatisfied with the campus physical plant and its administrative services. They also were dissatisfied with the food service and with health and recreational services. Like black students at predominantly white graduate schools, the students at predomi-nantly black graduate schools were dissatisfied with housing. While blacks at predominantly black schools liked the race relations cli-mate on campus and the racial diversity of the faculty, they had inadequate research opportunities to collaborate with faculty, and they were dissatisfied about this. But they were satisfied with their opportunities to serve as teaching assistants in predominantly black graduate schools.

In terms of social relationships, black graduate students in pre-dominantly black graduate schools were dissatisfied with their rate of participation in student organizations and in recreational activities; they were satisfied, however, with the friendliness of students at their schools. It could be that dissatisfaction with recreational and leisure-time activities is endemic to graduate student status, since African-American students at both predominantly white and predominantly black graduate schools had similar feelings. Probably, their studies are so pressing that insufficient time is available for nonacademic activities.

(*Continued on page 58*)

TABLE 6.1 Personal Adaptation to Graduate Study by Black Scholars in Predominantly White Graduate Schools

Campus Experience	Response		Response Distribution			
	Satisfied	Dis-satisfied	n	Mean	SD	Coeff. of Vartn
Competence of administration	•		45	3.49	0.73	21
Availability of study space	•		45	3.49	0.87	25
Quality of housing		•	39	1.95	1.57	81
Campus safety and security	•		44	3.11	1.02	33
Health services	•		44	2.73	1.58	58
Recreational facilities	•		45	2.69	1.58	59
Library services	•		44	3.52	0.90	26
Food service	•		41	2.76	1.26	46
Competency of faculty	•		46	3.46	0.59	17
Quality of instruction	•		45	3.22	0.93	29
Contact with faculty	•		45	2.96	0.98	33
Accessibility of advisor	•		46	3.15	1.23	39
Accessibility of dissertation faculty	•		44	2.95	1.35	46
Evaluation of students	•		46	3.02	1.02	34
Collaboration with faculty		•	45	2.49	1.31	53
Relationship with faculty of own race		•	44	1.89	0.92	49

	N	Mean	SD	%
Racial Diversity of faculty	45	1.89	0.86	49
Gender diversity of faculty	45	2.64	0.86	32
Competence of student body	45	3.24	0.68	21
Friendliness of students	46	2.96	0.97	33
Participation in student study group	46	2.37	1.27	54
Participation in graduate student organization	43	2.00	1.53	76
Participation in recreation	40	1.75	1.60	91
Student racial diversity	45	2.18	0.91	42
Relationship with students of own race	44	2.55	0.90	35
Race relations climate	45	2.27	1.12	40
Leadership among students	44	1.73	1.56	90
Meeting local community	42	2.14	1.41	66
Serving as teaching assistant	42	2.24	1.51	66
Serving as research assistant	41	1.83	1.45	79
Financial aid	45	2.67	1.33	50

Note. 1 = Very Dissatisfied
2 = Dissatisfied
3 = Satisfied
4 = Very Satisfied

Averages of 2.50 and below are classified as dissatisfied and 2.51 and above as satisfied.

TABLE 6.2 Personal Adaptation to Graduate Study by Black Scholars in Predominantly Black Graduate Schools

Campus Experience	Response		Response Distribution			
	Satisfied	Dis-satisfied	n	Mean	SD	Coeff. of Vartn
Competence of administration	•		5	3.60	0.55	15
Availability of study space	•		6	3.67	0.52	14
Quality of housing		•	5	1.40	1.34	96
Campus safety and security	•		6	2.67	1.37	51
Health services		•	6	1.00	1.55	155
Recreational facilities		•	6	1.83	1.72	94
Library services	•		6	3.33	0.52	15
Food service		•	6	2.17	1.72	79
Competency of faculty	•		6	3.17	0.75	24
Quality of instruction	•		6	3.17	0.75	24
Contact with faculty	•		6	2.67	1.37	51
Accessibility of advisor	•		6	3.17	0.75	24
Accessibility of dissertation faculty		•	6	2.17	1.72	79
Evaluation of students	•		6	3.33	0.52	15
Collaboration with faculty		•	6	1.83	1.47	80
Relationship with faculty of own race	•		6	3.17	0.75	24

Racial diversity of faculty	6	2.83	0.41	14
Gender diversity of faculty	6	3.00	---	---
Competence of student body	6	2.50	1.22	49
Friendliness of students	6	3.33	0.52	15
Participation in student study group	6	2.50	1.38	55
Participation in graduate student organization	5	1.40	1.34	96
Participation in recreation	6	1.33	1.51	113
Student racial diversity	6	2.83	0.41	14
Relationship with students of own race	6	2.83	0.41	14
Race relations climate	6	2.83	1.47	51
Leadership among students	6	0.50	1.22	245
Meeting local community	6	1.50	1.64	110
Serving as teaching assistant	6	3.16	0.41	13
Serving as research assistant	6	1.67	1.86	112
Financial aid	6	1.50	1.76	117

Note. 1 = Very Dissatisfied
      2 = Dissatisfied
      3 = Satisfied
      4 = Very Satisfied

Averages of 2.50 and below are classified as dissatisfied and 2.51 and above as satisfied.

ADAPTATION OF WHITE SCHOLARS
TO PREDOMINANTLY WHITE UNIVERSITIES

This study of 65 UNCF faculty scholars who participated in the Lilly/ UNCF Faculty Development Program includes eight white faculty members who were employed by historically black colleges. All eight attended predominantly white universities to complete their graduate studies while on leave from their official positions at UNCF institutions.

These white UNCF faculty scholars were asked to assess the social and academic climates of their schools of matriculation. The coding of responses was similar to the coding of black UNCF faculty scholars who participated in the fellowship program. The responses of both white scholars and black scholars who are similarly situated in terms of employment and financial sponsorship for graduate education should be of interest to decision makers at institutions of higher learning who are intent on increasing the success rate of all scholars in their graduate programs. Because these data on two different racial populations are available, a comparative analysis will be made to determine differences, if any, that exist in the adaptations that black scholars and white scholars made to their institutions of graduate study. Data for the responses of white scholars are included in Table 6.3.

Whites at predominantly white graduate schools were, in general, satisfied with the competence of their school's administration, faculty, and student body. Regarding administrative services and facilities such as campus security, library services, and recreational facilities, white scholars were satisfied. Their dissatisfactions centered largely on housing, health services, and food at their schools of matriculation. While white graduate scholars were satisfied with university recreational facilities, they nevertheless had limited leisure time and therefore were dissatisfied with opportunities to participate in campus recreational activities. However, they were satisfied with opportunities on campus to participate in student study groups. They did not feel isolated or alienated from these student-initiated academic opportunities.

The white scholars in the study expressed dissatisfaction with graduate student leadership on campus. This dissatisfaction could be a function of incompatible interests mediated by the age disparity between the Lilly/UNCF scholars and other graduate students. Most of the Lilly/UNCF scholars were over 40 years of age, married, and with children.

The white scholars associated with UNCF institutions probably were more sensitized to race relations issues than other majority-group graduate students at predominantly white graduate schools. They were dissatisfied with the race relations climate on campus and with the limited representation of minority professors on the faculty. The college faculties in their institutions of employment were diversified. Usually, this was not the case in the predominantly white graduate schools where the scholars matriculated.

While these white scholars from UNCF colleges who studied in predominantly white institutions were aware of the presence of racial discrimination, they reported having had good personal experiences with faculty and other students on campus. They were satisfied with contacts they had developed with faculty members in general and their advisors in particular. They collaborated with faculty on various academic projects and were often chosen as teaching assistants. Since most white scholars in the Lilly/UNCF program were employed by small liberal arts colleges, they were less oriented to research and tended to miss out on opportunities to serve as research assistants. However, opportunities to serve as teaching assistants and other sources of funding were sufficient to meet the costs of graduate study. Thus, white scholars in this study were satisfied with financial aid and other fiscal-support arrangements.

The experiences of the white scholars in predominantly white graduate schools were similar to those of black scholars in similar schools in some important respects. Both black scholars and white scholars were satisfied with the competence of the faculty members and the administrative officers of their schools of matriculation. Moreover, all were dissatisfied with housing for graduate students. This could be explained, in part, by the age, marital, and parental status of this group. As noted above, the Lilly/UNCF scholars were more likely than their fellow students to be older, married, and parents of school-aged children; consequently, their housing needs would be different from those of single students.

The most serious difference between the scholars associated with the two racial populations had to do with their relationship with faculty members in predominantly white institutions. The white graduate scholars had easy access to their teachers and often were chosen as teaching assistants. This was not the experience of black scholars on such campuses. Moreover, black graduate students complained that student study groups were not accessible to them at predominantly white graduate schools. Such groups were available to white graduate students.

(*Continued on page 62*)

TABLE 6.3 Personal Adaptation to Graduate Study by White Scholars in Predominantly White Graduate Schools

Campus Experience	Response		Response Distribution			
	Satisfied	Dis-satisfied	n	Mean	SD	Coeff. of Vartn
Competence of administration	•		8	3.25	0.71	22
Availability of study space	•		8	3.25	1.16	36
Quality of housing		•	8	1.63	1.77	109
Campus safety and security	•		8	2.75	1.49	54
Health services		•	8	2.00	1.69	84
Recreational facilities	•		8	3.13	1.36	43
Library services	•		8	3.50	0.53	15
Food service		•	7	2.43	1.40	58
Competency of faculty	•		8	3.38	0.52	15
Quality of instruction	•		8	3.50	0.76	22
Contact with faculty	•		8	3.63	0.52	14
Accessibility of advisor	•		8	3.38	0.74	22
Accessibility of dissertation faculty	•		8	3.50	0.53	15
Evaluation of students	•		8	3.63	0.52	14
Collaboration with faculty	•		8	3.00	1.41	47
Relationship with faculty of own race	•		8	3.00	1.31	44

	n	M	SD	%
Racial diversity of faculty	8	2.38	0.92	39
Gender diversity of faculty	8	3.00	0.76	25
Competence of student body	8	3.13	0.64	21
Friendliness of students	8	3.00	0.93	31
Participation in student study group	8	2.63	1.69	64
Participation in graduate student organization	8	3.25	0.46	14
Participation in recreation	8	2.13	1.81	85
Student racial diversity	8	2.63	0.92	35
Relationship with students of own race	8	3.00	1.31	44
Race relations climate	8	2.50	1.20	48
Leadership among students	8	2.50	1.41	57
Meeting local community	8	2.75	1.75	64
Serving as teaching assistant	8	4.00	---	---
Serving as research assistant	8	2.50	1.69	68
Financial aid	7	3.29	1.50	46

Note. 1 = Very Dissatisfied
2 = Dissatisfied
3 = Satisfied
4 = Very Satisfied

Averages of 2.50 and below are classified as dissatisfied and 2.51 and above as satisfied.

Neither blacks nor whites in graduate school had sufficient time to participate in recreational activities. Whites had support systems, such as student organizations on campus, in which to participate. These, reportedly, were not as accessible to black graduate students.

PATTERNS OF ASSOCIATION BETWEEN FACETS OF THE GRADUATE SCHOOL EXPERIENCE

The matrix of correlation coefficients presented in Table 6.4 provides insight into those experiences that all Lilly/UNCF scholars believe are important in a campus community. The population of scholars is multiracial but predominantly black. This presentation examines factors such as faculty competence, the quality of the academic program, student–faculty interaction, presence of racial/ethnic diversity on campus, participation in university organizations, and opportunities to serve as research or teaching assistants.

As mentioned earlier, both black and white graduate scholars are pleased with the competence of the faculty and the administration in their schools of matriculation. These scholars see a direct link between an able administration and a competent faculty. The correlation coefficient between these two is .69. This fact means that, in the

TABLE 6.4 Correlation Matrix of Campus Experiences of a 65-Person Population

CAMPUS EXPERIENCE	1	2	3	4	5	6	7	8
1. Competence of administration	1.00	.30	.20	.21	.69	.44	.31	.21
2. Quality of housing	.29	1.00	.40	.30	.27	.24	.21	.27
3. Health services	.20	.40	1.00	.46	.38	.33	.19	.16
4. Recreational facilities	.21	.30	.48	1.00	.29	.42	.17	.10
5. Competence of faculty	.69	.27	.38	.29	1.00	.59	.41	.24
6. Quality of instruction	.44	.24	.33	.42	.59	1.00	.33	.24
7. Contact with faculty	.31	.21	.19	.17	.41	.33	1.00	.24
8. Access to advisor	.21	.27	.16	.10	.24	.24	.24	1.00
9. Access to thesis committee	.09	.15	.17	.39	.32	.15	.26	.44
10. Evaluation of students	.49	.23	.16	.18	.35	.46	.32	.52
11. Collaboration with faculty	.12	.28	.31	.25	.21	.24	.34	.14
12. Intrarace relations, faculty	.00	.01	.05	-.04	.12	-.04	.14	.14
13. Racial diversity of faculty	.15	.08	-.06	-.04	.21	.08	.11	.07
14. Competence of students	.39	.16	.16	.28	.53	.31	.40	.23
15. Friendliness of students	.40	.21	.00	.12	.37	.26	.36	.43
16. Participation, study groups	.27	.30	.31	.37	.34	.32	.38	.45
17. Participation, recreation	.03	.22	.36	.59	.18	.35	.20	.23
18. Racial diversity of students	.25	.02	.02	.13	.23	.14	.09	.06
19. Intrarace relations, students	.09	.03	.06	.05	.01	.16	.08	.09
20. Race relations climate	.24	.20	.21	.43	.35	.51	.30	.23
21. Serving, teaching assistant	.16	.14	.06	.22	.18	.28	.29	.08
22. Serving, research assistant	.29	.37	.42	.39	.31	.24	.35	.16

opinion of these scholars, nearly half of the variance in faculty quality may be attributed to competent administrative action. Indeed, this sample of multiracial, predominantly black scholars indicated that they believe that there is a greater association between administrative competence and a quality faculty than there is between administrative action and any other service or function of the university.

The scholars in this study also asserted that an association exists between the competent performance of graduate students and the quality of their faculty members. The correlation coefficient between these two variables is .53.

One component of competence, according to these scholars, is the capacity of instructors to evaluate minority group students fairly. The correlation coefficient between teacher competence and the fair-evaluation-of-students variable is .35. Moreover, our sample of scholars would assign to the administration an oversight responsibility to guarantee fair treatment of students, as indicated by the coefficient of .49 that resulted from the intercorrelation of administrative competence and the fair-evaluation-of-students variables.

This analysis suggests that there is a series of functions that must be performed by individuals in graduate education who fill different status positions. As a collectivity, these multiracial scholars believed that the administration is responsible for assembling a good faculty

Composed of Black Scholars Enrolled in Predominantly White Graduate Schools

9	10	11	12	13	14	15	16	17	18	19	20	21	22
.09	.49	.12	.00	.15	.39	.40	.27	.03	.25	.10	.24	.16	.29
.15	.23	.28	.02	.08	.16	.22	.30	.22	.02	.03	.20	.14	.37
.17	.16	.31	-.05	-.06	.16	.00	.31	.36	.02	.06	.21	.06	.42
.39	.18	.25	-.04	-.04	.28	.13	.37	.59	.13	.05	.43	.22	.39
.32	.35	.21	.12	.21	.53	.38	.35	.18	.23	.01	.35	.18	.31
.15	.46	.24	-.04	.08	.31	.26	.32	.35	.14	-.16	.51	.28	.24
.26	.32	.34	.14	.11	.40	.36	.38	.20	.09	.08	.28	.29	.35
.44	.52	.14	.15	.07	.23	.43	.46	.23	.06	.09	.23	.07	.16
1.00	.11	.10	.04	.09	.24	.18	.31	.26	-.01	.00	.24	.12	.28
.11	1.00	.31	.20	.23	.21	.28	.47	.15	.36	.21	.25	.33	.25
.10	.31	1.00	.32	.19	.29	.33	.45	.29	.11	.19	.25	.36	.47
.04	.20	.32	1.00	.71	-.02	.33	.27	.01	.40	.47	.20	.39	.37
.09	.23	.19	.71	1.00	.05	.20	.27	-.04	.44	.33	.28	.18	.21
.24	.21	.29	-.02	.05	1.00	.31	.39	.22	.07	-.01	.21	-.03	.22
.18	.28	.33	.33	.20	.31	1.00	.37	.07	.22	.17	.31	.18	.28
.31	.47	.45	.27	.27	.39	.37	1.00	.39	.10	.02	.34	.15	.39
.26	.15	.29	.01	-.04	.22	.07	.39	1.00	.02	-.01	.27	.11	.17
-.01	.36	.11	.37	.44	.07	.22	.10	.02	1.00	.70	.53	.19	.24
.00	.21	.19	.47	.33	-.01	.17	.02	-.01	.70	1.00	.37	.07	.30
.24	.25	.25	.20	.28	.21	.31	.34	.27	.53	.37	1.00	.18	.16
.12	.33	.36	.39	.18	-.03	.18	.15	.11	.19	.07	.18	1.00	.50
.28	.25	.47	.37	.21	.22	.28	.39	.17	.24	.30	.16	.50	1.00

and that a quality teaching staff contributes to a competent student body. The hierarchy stated above differs from that which derives the reputation of a school from the quality of students admitted.

Obviously, there are many factors other than teaching competence that enhance learning in a university setting. Two-thirds of the variance in the student competence factor could be explained by these other factors. Nevertheless, a substantial explanation is discovered when one-third of the variance in the distribution of one factor is attributable to the distribution of another. This is precisely what the correlation coefficient of .53 between faculty competence and student competence reveals.

The scholars in this study believed that the race relations climate on campus is influenced in a positive way by the quality of instruction offered by the faculty. A correlation coefficient of .51 between these two variables is significant. From this study emerges a new criterion of teacher competence—the contribution that a teacher makes to a positive experience of intergroup relations in the campus community. This finding is similar to one reported elsewhere. An analysis of the criteria of outstanding professional status offered by 152 black scholars in a study conducted in the 1980s revealed that, in their collective judgment, an individual who is callous about oppression and indifferent or uncommitted to the people who experience it should not be considered an outstanding scholar (Willie, 1986).

Most of the Lilly/UNCF white scholars as well as most of the black scholars in this study were dissatisfied with the racial diversity of the teaching faculty in their predominantly white graduate schools. They believed that more faculty diversity would tend to result in more diversity among students. Their belief that an association existed between student diversity and faculty diversity resulted in a correlation coefficient of .44 between these two variables. Based on these data, it is reasonable to conclude that a university that wishes to have a diversified student body should guard against recruiting a faculty that is homogeneous. The achievement of a diversified student body requires many different initiatives, among which is hiring a faculty that is heterogeneous in its characteristics.

One educational benefit of a diversified faculty for African-American students is the increased possibility of their bonding with campus professionals such as faculty members and working with faculty as teaching assistants. In predominantly black graduate schools, where faculties were more diversified than elsewhere, the African-American scholars in this study were satisfied with their opportunity to serve as teaching assistants. But in predominantly white graduate schools, where there was less faculty diversity, African-American scholars tended to have fewer chances to serve as teaching assistants. The correlation coefficient of .39 between student relationships with faculty of their own racial group and the opportunity to serve as teaching assistants suggests that the latter kind of student–teacher involvement depends in part on the presence of teachers of a racial group that is similar to that of the students.

The scholars in this study indicated that a diversified student body contributes to a better race relations climate on campus. A correlation coefficient of .53 indicates that, in the opinion of the scholars who responded to the questionnaire, a significant portion of the variance in campus race relations is associated with student body diversity. Obviously, experiences other than student body diversity contribute to the condition of race relations in a university community. But population diversity is an important contribution to a good race relations campus climate. It very well could be the essential experience in intergroup relations, without which little else of positive value can happen.

When there is diversity in a student population, scholars not only have the privilege of encountering others whose ways of life are different from their own and learning from them, but also seem to get along better with students of their own racial group. In this study, at least half of the variance in intragroup relations (getting along well with students of one's own race) was influenced by intergroup relationships (campus student diversity). These two variables intercorrelated at .70. This finding suggests that one may come to understand oneself better by seeking to know others better. This finding may be stated as a principle that intrapersonal intelligence and interpersonal intelligence complement each other and are mutually enhancing.

SUMMARY

In summary, blacks in predominantly white graduate schools are satisfied with the competence of their administrative, teaching, and student colleagues in these schools. They are particularly satisfied with the quality of instruction but wish that there were more diversity in the student body and faculty. Blacks in predominantly white academic settings are unhappy with their access to teachers, particularly opportunities to serve as teaching and research assistants. And, in general, they are discomforted by the race relations climate on campus.

Blacks in predominantly black graduate schools also are satisfied with the competence of the faculty but are less satisfied with the competence of their student colleagues. They like the diversity of the teaching staff and find the students friendly at these schools. Blacks in predominantly black graduate schools are also pleased with the opportunities they have to serve as teaching assistants. In general, they classify as favorable the race relations climate on predominantly black college campuses.

With reference to predominantly white graduate schools, the main supportive actions that they may undertake for black graduate students is to increase the number of black faculty and black students on campus. Blackwell (1987) called attention to this phenomenon when he observed that the hiring of more black teachers is one of the best support systems that can be provided for black students at white colleges.

7 Mentoring Relationships

Mentoring for minorities is in need of much study. As pointed out in Chapter 3, Levinson (1978) stated that women and minorities experience greater difficulty than others in finding mentors. Some studies have indicated that mentors may be key in advancing the careers of their proteges (Willie, 1987). The functions of mentors, according to Levinson (1978), are to sponsor, guide, and provide counsel and support to their proteges. He also assigned the mentor a developmental task, that of "facilitating the realization of the dream," and called this responsibility "the most crucial one" (p. 98). The mentor does this by believing in a protege and giving his or her blessings to risky experiments that the protege may wish to attempt. Even more important than these functions, the mentor must be willing to sacrifice, if necessary, in behalf of a protege, suffer his or her failures and disappointments, and rejoice in incremental successes as well as final victories.

With these demanding and multiple requirements of mentoring, one can understand why mentors are in short supply. Yet their presence is essential in helping young African-American and other minority scholars through periods of doubt and indecision. When the distinguished black historian, John Hope Franklin, doubted whether he would go to Harvard for graduate study because his family's finances had been decimated by the Depression, his mentor, Professor T. S. Currier of Fisk University, insisted that money would not keep Franklin from going to Harvard. Unable to find sufficient funding from any source, Currier, who incidentally was white, "went to the bank and borrowed enough money to pay for Franklin's first year at Harvard" (Willie, 1986, p. 18). This is a beautiful example of a mentor sacrificing in behalf of his protege.

Beyond personal support like that illustrated above, mentors sometimes "provide a link of trust between individuals and institutions" for black students (Willie, 1987, p. 99). This may involve an intercessory function—"insisting that rules, regulations, and procedures are applied fairly and that the full participation of proteges

in complex [institutional] systems [is] not impeded in any way"
(pp. 103–104).

DATA FROM THE STUDY

The data in Table 7.1 indicate that it is a "toss-up" as to whether
faculty scholars in United Negro College Fund institutions will experience a mentoring relationship while pursuing a graduate degree:
53% had mentors and 47% did not. Given the importance of mentors,
half of the black scholars in this study may have been disadvantaged
because they did not have mentors. Nearly one-fifth of the participants in this study wanted a mentor but could not find one. Some
scholars did not want or need mentors. However, the proportion of all
scholars who felt no need for a mentor was less than 10% of the total.

Of all mentors, it is interesting to note that nearly half (46%) were
based in institutions other than the graduate school in which the faculty
scholar matriculated. This is a remarkable finding in that the scholar's
institution of employment (and not the school of matriculation) was the
setting in which nearly 1 out of every 2 mentors was found. When the
scholars who did not have mentors are added to those who found
mentors in settings other than their matriculating institutions, one
observes that the graduate school of matriculation provided mentors for
only one-fourth of all the faculty scholars in this study.

There is a wide dispersion of areas of expertise represented in the
mentor pool. Though not directly evident from summary data presented in Table 7.1, it should be noted that the fields of specialization
of the mentors do not necessarily correspond to the scholars' fields of
study; in fact, a sizable proportion of the scholars have mentors
outside their own disciplines. Probably, such relationships are engen-
dered outside traditional adviser–advisee associations.

MATCHING STUDENTS WITH MENTORS

We have no conclusive evidence, but it appears that individuals tend
to link up with mentors whose personal characteristics are similar to
their own. We make this assertion because predominantly white colleges and universities in which most of the scholars studied have
faculties in which minorities, and especially African-American minorities, are less than 5% of the total number of faculty members; yet,
4 out of every 10 of the UNCF faculty scholars had blacks as their

TABLE 7.1 Role of Mentor in Faculty Fellowship Experience

Characteristics of Mentor	n	%
Presence		
Yes	34	53.1
No	30	46.9
Total	64	100.0
Sex		
Male	23	69.7
Female	10	30.3
Total	33	100.0
Race		
White	20	60.6
Black	13	39.4
Total	33	100.0
Field		
Social Science	8	24.2
Education	8	24.2
Business	1	3.0
Mathematics and Sciences	3	9.1
Humanities	13	39.4
Total	33	100.0
Affiliation		
Institution of Employment	14	40.0
Doctoral Institution	19	54.3
Undergraduate Institution	1	2.9
Other	1	2.9
Total	35	100.0
Why No Mentor		
No Perceived Need	6	30.0
Wanted but Could Not Find	12	60.0
Other	2	10.0
Total	20	100.0

mentors. If there is a tendency toward same-race selection for mentors and proteges, then colleges and universities that encourage diversity in their student bodies should insist on diversity in their faculties so that mentors are available for a range of students.

While the data in Table 7.1 suggest a modest same-race or same-gender tendency in mentoring, there nevertheless is evidence that whites may be mentors to blacks and that males may be mentors to females. Indeed, 61% of the mentors in this study were white, and 70% were male; yet a majority of faculty scholars were black and female.

Evidence that the mentor functions as a support system as well as a role model was revealed in the analysis of cross-gender and cross-race mentoring. As shown in Table 7.2, 6 out of every 10 graduate scholars with a mentor were female, but only 3 out of every 10 of the mentors were female. Concerning race (see Table 7.3), about 9 out of every 10 graduate scholars in this study who had a mentor were black, but 6 out of every 10 mentors were black. These data reveal that women graduate students tended to have slightly greater access to men as mentors than blacks had to whites as mentors.

INTERPRETATION

In *Mainstreaming Outsiders*, Blackwell (1987) reports that the hiring of blacks for faculty and administrative positions in traditionally white institutions should be a matter of the highest priority. He makes this assertion because his research has demonstrated that the presence of black faculty is the most powerful predictor of enrollment and graduation of blacks from professional schools. Blackwell concludes that "black students want and need black mentors," for the evidence "is compelling" (p. 359).

We arrived at the same conclusion based on an examination of the very high correlation coefficient of .71 for similar variables in our study (refer to Table 6.4). Since racially diversified college and university faculties tend to include a substantial number of African-Amer-

TABLE 7.2 Mentor-Scholar Association Cross-tabulated by Sex

	Sex of Scholar					
	Female		Male		Total	
Sex of Mentor	n	%	n	%	n	%
Female	7	35.0	4	28.6	11	32.4
Male	13	65.0	10	71.4	23	67.6
Total	20	100.0	14	100.0	34	100.0

TABLE 7.3 Mentor-Scholar Association Cross-tabulated by Race

| | Race of Scholar | | | | | |
| Race of Mentor | Black | | White | | Total | |
	n	%	n	%	n	%
Black	18	58.1	2	66.7	20	58.8
White	13	41.9	1	33.3	14	41.2
Total	31	100.0	3	100.0	34	100.0

ican professors, there is a higher probability that these faculty members will serve as mentors for black graduate students. Whites may serve as mentors for black graduate students too. But the probability that black students will find mentors among whites is lower than the probability that black professors will assume a mentoring responsibility for such students.

Because black graduate students have a higher probability of finding mentors among black professors and because so few blacks are employed as faculty and staff by predominantly white institutions, only one-fourth of the graduate scholars in this study had mentors in the institutions in which they studied for a doctoral degree. This finding supports the observation that the hiring of faculty of color should be a matter of the highest priority to support students of color.

In Table 6.4 the other high correlation coefficient (.70) was the response of study participants to questions about relationships with students of their own race and the racial diversity of the student body. On college and university campuses that were racially diversified, black graduate students tended to have a better relationship with other black students. These relationships may reflect student-to-student mentoring, when the availability of mentoring professors of the same race as students is insufficient. Blackwell (1987) found that "black students . . . need . . . a critical mass of black graduate and professional school students, sufficient to enable them to form viable networks" (p. 359). This finding is similar to one reported in an earlier study, *Black Students at White Colleges* (Willie & McCord, 1972), that "a small number of blacks on campus [are condemned] to an inadequate social life and intraracial as well as interracial discord" (p. 109). On the basis of these findings, one may conclude that the quality of academic life as well as "the quality of campus social life for blacks is directly related to the number of black students enrolled" (p. 15).

The availability of mentoring is an important component in the quality of campus life for blacks and other minorities. The mentor provides the link of trust between individuals and institutions and nurtures both until they embrace each other. The mentor does this by accepting his or her protege as worthy of esteem and insisting that institutions be fair.

To get close to another as required of one who is a mentor means making oneself vulnerable. As Blackwell (1983) has stated, "the mentor–protege dyad is often charged" with emotion because of differences in age and status of the participants (p. 12). Because of this and other characteristics of the relationship, mentors and proteges must mutually agree to work together. Mentors, unlike advisors, cannot be assigned to specific students. Advisors may become mentors, but many advisor–advisee associations never evolve to the mentor–protege relationship.

Essential in the evolution of a mentor–protege relationship is the element of trust. Responsibility for initiating a trusting relationship is that of the dominant person. It is he or she who must certify that the relationship is safe from exploitation. Because race has been a major source of interpersonal estrangement in human society, mentoring relationships of trust tend to occur more frequently among members of the same race. However, they do not have to be this way, as the long-term mentoring relationship between black historian John Hope Franklin and white historian T. S. Currier has demonstrated (Willie, 1986).

8 Summary, Conclusions, and Implications

SUMMARY

Scholars who responded to surveys in this study average 10 years of UNCF teaching experience. Over 70% received baccalaureate degrees from either a private or public historically black college. These facts suggest the presence of institutional loyalty to UNCF and other predominantly black schools among faculty scholars who received grants for graduate study.

These faculty scholars are persistent in their pursuit of graduate education. Ninety-five percent of all who had not completed degree requirements expressed firm intentions of finishing. A majority had pursued graduate studies 5 years or longer.

Doctoral Status of Scholars

Faculty scholars were almost evenly divided into three degree-status categories: 26% were enrolled in classes or had just completed course work; 39% were writing qualifying papers or theses; and 35% had completed requirements for the doctorate. Most scholars in the last category had received doctoral degrees and were continuing to teach in UNCF institutions.

A large percentage of spouses of married scholars were pursuing graduate-level education or had received graduate degrees. One might conjecture that a highly educated spouse provides incentive for a wife or husband to attain a similar level of education.

Some differences existed between scholars who had completed their degree requirements and those who were still in progress. Scholars who had completed study for the doctorate degree in a timely fashion tended to receive higher grades in their graduate courses than scholars who required a longer period of time. However, the absence of disparity between these two groups in undergraduate academic records suggests that important individual changes after matriculation to graduate study facilitated or impeded doctoral study. More-

73

over, this finding also calls into question the reliability of under-graduate records as predictors of the capacity of African-American scholars to complete the requirements for advanced degrees.

Financial Assistance of Faculty Scholars

Half of all faculty scholars had to supplement income from their financial aid package with income from additional work while en-rolled in a doctoral program; 40% worked in excess of 20 hours per week. Without doubt, the need to work interfered with the timely completion of doctoral study.

Scholars received an average financial aid package from all sources just in excess of $29,000 during their entire period of doctoral study. These funds were exhausted in 1 to 2 years of study. Many scholars had to earn funds through work to finish their graduate programs.

Sixty-three percent of the scholars did not receive a grant from any source after their fourth year of doctoral study. Yet 83% of all scholars required more than 4 years to complete their doctorates. Thus, most scholars were required to finance the latter years of graduate study either from family resources, personal loans, or in-come derived from working while matriculating in school.

Campus Relationships

Black scholars in graduate school on predominantly white cam-puses reported a high level of satisfaction with the competence of the administration and faculty at their degree-granting institutions. How-ever, the black scholars attending these schools were more satisfied with administrative services than with faculty relationships.

A strong intercorrelation was observed between the variables of racial diversity of faculty and the opportunity for interaction with faculty of one's own race. Most black graduate students were men-tored by members of their own race, although effective mentoring did occur across racial and gender categories.

CONCLUSIONS

Based on data analyzed in this study, we may conclude that faculty development programs are significant in helping scholars affiliated with predominantly black private colleges and universities to attain doctoral degrees.

The scholars who received fellowships for graduate study have great motivation and the capacity to endure. They performed well in their schools of matriculation and proceeded to complete their degrees; however, the average scholar required more than 4 years to finish all degree requirements.

The length of time required to complete a degree is, in part, a function of the absence of support for continuing study beyond 2 to 3 years. While foundation grants accounted for nearly three-quarters of the grant assistance that these scholars received, clearly the grants were insufficient to cover total educational expenses and in most instances were terminated before they could have maximum effect.

Full financial support from the first through the fourth or fifth year of graduate study probably would shorten the period of study and increase the degree-completion rate of black scholars. Foundation sponsorship is essential since African-American graduate scholars, by their own testimony, have limited access to campus-based sources of funding such as research and teaching assistantships.

Beyond programs that assist teachers in predominantly black private colleges and universities to attain doctoral degrees, attention should be directed toward ways of retaining fully credentialed scholars on the faculty and staff of these institutions. Those who complete doctoral degrees are eligible for advancements in rank in UNCF institutions, but more must be done to limit the competition between these colleges and other institutions for talented and well-educated UNCF staff. Increasing the obligation of faculty scholars from a payback period of 2 years of service for *all* fellowship assistance received, to a payback period of 2 years in any UNCF college for *each year* of fellowship assistance received, may enhance the retention rate at UNCF institutions of faculty who benefitted from foundation-sponsored programs for graduate study. Under this condition, faculty scholars who received 4 to 5 years of financial support could be obligated to serve any UNCF school for 8 to 10 years as a way of discharging the payback obligation.

In addition to increasing the number of years over which UNCF institutions could expect to receive the services of scholars who became fully credentialed through faculty development programs, the extended payback arrangement would make faculty and staff at UNCF colleges less attractive to competing institutions at the end of their period of obligated service. This is because those scholars would be among the better-compensated faculty and staff, for whom competing employers would have to outbid the UNCF institutions. The recommended extended payback period of service would bring both justice and equity to the process of retention and recruitment of minority faculty in the nation's system of higher education.

Finally, this study indicates that predominantly white colleges and universities must undertake deliberate efforts to make the campuses of graduate schools more hospitable to African-American and other minority scholars. Inservice education programs are needed to help white faculty members learn how to serve effectively as mentors for minorities. Moreover, black and other minority students need increased opportunities to serve as research and teaching assistants with faculty. In general, the black scholars in this study said that opportunities to collaborate with faculty in intellectual activities outside the classroom were inadequate.

Most black students are displeased with the race relations climate of the graduate schools that they attend. They are dissatisfied with their participation in graduate student groups, including study groups and recreational groups. Because these graduate scholars have little, if any, opportunity to meet community people in areas where graduate schools are located, they are dependent on the campus for social as well as academic support.

The graduate scholars in this study believed that their dissatisfactions might be diminished if the critical mass of black and other minority students enrolled and the black and other minority faculty and administrators employed were increased. But the proportions of such populations were extremely small at most graduate schools. These schools must implement affirmative action recruitment and retention policies and practices immediately to partially meet the academic and social support needs of their minority students.

INCREASING THE MINORITY GRADUATION RATE IN DOCTORAL PROGRAMS

The evidence from this study supports the position that the chances of successful degree-completion for black doctoral candidates are enhanced if a strong bond exists between the students and their institution. The conditions for this bonding to occur include providing opportunities for scholars to establish an adequate base of financial support, promoting the development of relationships between students and faculty, and strengthening the network among students. If present, these features will permit students to develop a bond with their university, thereby increasing their chances of graduating in a timely manner and returning to their schools of employment with enhanced personal and professional skills.

Providing Baseline Financial Security

Findings from this study indicate that some students fall under inexorable financial pressure within the first 4 years of graduate study. They often seek outside employment to pay tuition and fees, as well as to fulfill normal family obligations. In many cases, these students secure employment in areas far afield from their academic interests. Complicating this is the fact that job responsibilities force many students to reduce the amount of time they devote to course work or writing. Thus, this process of physical and academic disengagement from the doctoral program diminishes the chances that students will complete degree requirements in a timely fashion. Not only is development of a psychological bond with the university impeded when scholars must seek employment away from campus, but lack of regular contact with faculty also reduces the chances that students will develop mentoring or sponsorship association with established scholars.

Universities should strive to assemble financial aid packages for African-American and other minority graduate students that will provide a baseline of support for 4 to 5 years of the students' period of study. Providing a package of government grants, loans, work-study incentives, and funds from university and private sources will serve at least two purposes. First, it will allow graduate students to make a smooth transition from full-time participation in the labor force to student status. For many of the black doctoral students in this study, this transition also required adaptation from predominantly black settings in which they were among the racial majority to environments in which they were members of a racial minority. Sensitivity to the magnitude of the adaptations required by these circumstances is needed.

Second, this 4- to 5-year funding guarantee would allow students to develop a network of contacts, both student and faculty, which might then lead to alternative sources of financial support through teaching and research assistantships in the students' areas of disciplinary interest. Through this network students might identify sources of financial support, including teaching and research assistantships for the fourth or fifth year of study and beyond. Obviously, the university must give greater support to minority students in their search for additional sources of financial assistance, both internal and external to the educational institution.

Mentoring

The data from the Lilly/UNCF study showed that a comparatively low number of these graduate students established a meaningful mentoring relationship with a resident faculty member. Half of all students in the study reported having a mentor, yet only 1 out of every 2 students who experienced such a relationship identified the mentor as a member of the student's institution of graduate study.

The presence of a faculty mentor or faculty sponsor in the graduate school setting offers the student many advantages, both personal and academic. Access to an established scholar provides the student with opportunities to test new hypotheses and research plans, affording the student a decided edge in his or her development as a bona fide scholar. A faculty mentor can lead a protege to sources of academic support, including colleagues, and to literature relevant to the student's research interest. A mentor relationship can also provide opportunities for research and publishing and participation in programs of professional associations.

The self-concept of students and their sense of legitimacy within the broader community of scholars are also enhanced through collegial interaction with a faculty mentor. Students attain a sense of confirmation in receiving positive feedback from a faculty member and being treated as colleagues. On a more practical level, a faculty sponsor can lead a fledgling graduate student to sources of financial support. Not only will collaboration on a funded project of the sponsoring professor provide students with financial backing and keep them engaged in work relevant to their study, but the students will also establish a foothold in their research field by learning some of the trade secrets from a trustworthy source. All of these activities contribute to the bonding between students and their school, a process that increases the chances that they will remain active, engaged scholars through and after graduation.

One step that can be taken to promote the development of mentoring relationships is to encourage faculty to reach out to students through informal contacts, such as dinners for new students in faculty homes. The institution should also be flexible in approving student requests to change advisors if a student has identified a particular professor with whom he or she wishes to work. Random assignment of new students to faculty advisors is not likely to accomplish much more than perfunctory advisory duties, such as orientation to university procedures, approving study plans, advising on course selections, and so forth. Students should also be encouraged to take independent study or field experience course work that involves collaboration with both university and community contact persons. It is conceivable that mentors might come from the community setting, which, while not a source preferable to the university faculty (for the reasons discussed above), might create valuable professional contacts in the larger community.

Enhancing Student Relationships

The preponderance of the data from the Lilly/UNCF study suggests that black students enrolled in predominantly white graduate programs are troubled by many aspects of campus life. These findings lead to the conclusion that many minority scholars are isolated from the mainstream of their university life. In the most severe cases, this isolation leads to the student's withdrawal from the program, often without having made sufficient progress toward a final degree.

Just as the university must make efforts to promote linkages between faculty and students, so must students have the chance to develop support networks among themselves. One way for the university to further both of these goals is by providing funds for small-scale research projects that students may undertake with the supervision of faculty members. A group of students matched with a professor with similar research interests could work to develop additional research projects, and identify potential funding sources, while concurrently providing each other with intellectual and interpersonal support during the pressure points of the graduate school experience.

Summary

To a large extent, a student's chances of persisting through a rigorous course of doctoral studies are determined by the strength of his or her bond with an individual faculty member and with fellow students. This bond allows the doctoral candidate to remain engaged in consistent, serious research relevant to his or her thesis topic. In cases where personal responsibilities draw a student away from the academic setting, the linkage weakens, as does the probability that the student will proceed smoothly through the program and graduate. The three components discussed above are offered as a means for universities to take steps to strengthen the bond between African-American graduate students and other members of the academic community.

The cohort of scholars from the Lilly/UNCF study exhibited a history of a deep sense of loyalty to historically black institutions. Some of these individuals hold faculty appointments at the UNCF institution from which they earned an undergraduate degree. Many others are alumni of historically black colleges. Some of these scholars have worked for many years in various capacities at their UNCF institutions.

Data from this study suggest that this group of scholars possesses a sense of institutional fealty that in the past was generalizable to other settings. Yet these same individuals expressed only limited success at developing satisfying relationships in their graduate programs at predominantly white universities. Many minority scholars simply need the proper set of circumstances to fulfill their scholarly interests. Without institutional support many of these students will remain largely on the periphery; for others, this sense of isolation will grow so strong as to drive them from their doctoral studies. It is the duty of the university to create the conditions—financial, interpersonal, intellectual—that in combination will promote the timely completion of doctoral degrees for minority scholars.

IMPLICATIONS FOR
A NATIONAL HIGHER EDUCATION POLICY

As the nation becomes increasingly aware of the need to enlarge its pool of teaching and research scholars who have earned doctoral degrees, attention should be targeted on blacks and other minority groups. They represent an underdeveloped resource. Our study indicates that the recruitment methods for blacks should probably differ from recruitment methods for whites because, among other reasons, undergraduate academic performance in terms of grade-point averages is a less reliable way of determining the capacity of minority students to successfully complete graduate studies. The black graduate students in this study outperformed their own undergraduate records. Certainly, the selectivity of the schools from which blacks received baccalaureate degrees should not be used in graduate admissions decisions. Most of these scholars who had graduate study averages of B+ or better attended predominantly black schools in the

South, many of which are not listed in guides to college publications as "very selective."

Because of the absence of opportunities in the past, some blacks who have the potential to become teaching and research scholars have found initial employment in public school systems or in public service occupations. Recruitment efforts for black graduate students, therefore, should extend beyond colleges and universities. The traditional methods of recruitment for graduate study among students who concentrated in academic disciplines probably omit many promising black candidates. Social work and public school teaching were typical sources from which many of the scholars in this study were drawn; such sources should be turned to for new recruits for graduate study in the learned disciplines.

The vast majority of black scholars in this study who successfully earned their doctorates obtained degrees in the humanities, education, and the social sciences. Only 7% specialized in mathematics and science, while clearly twice as many could have done so based on aptitude and previous interest. With an increasingly technology-dominated economy in the United States, it is imperative that an increased number of blacks and other minorities, who will be an increasing proportion of the national labor force, be encouraged to receive terminal degrees in mathematics, science, and technical fields.

The most rapidly growing population sector in the United States today is that of racial and ethnic minority groups. In order to maintain the nation's human resource needs in several technical fields, it will be necessary to identify and cultivate black and other minority talent at early ages. Emphasis must be placed on encouraging blacks to stay in these fields after receiving master's degrees. To do so, clearer identification of career opportunities and rewards in science and mathematics must be shared with minority-group students in high school and college and with students in training for first-level graduate degrees.

This study also has implications regarding the financing of graduate education for African-Americans and other minority groups. Foundations prefer to initiate programs and then turn them over to other sources for funding their continuation. While this may be a wise and responsible way of expending limited philanthropic resources for public service programs in general, it is a contraindicated policy for financing graduate study for black and other minority students. This study reveals that resources tend to be terminated for black graduate students precisely at the time when they need financing most to complete graduate studies. Many fellowship and grant programs are limited to 3 years or less. Fourth-, fifth-, and sixth-year grants or fellowships are definitely needed but seldom available. Such support would substantially increase the number of black and other minority students who receive doctoral degrees through efforts like the Lilly/ UNCF Faculty Development Program. Since minority professionals need to be fully credentialed to effectively compete with others for responsible positions in the labor force, grant and fellowship programs that do not offer support beyond the third year of graduate study condemn many minority professionals to a permanent, unfinished, all-but-dissertation status. Such individuals, most of whom are first-generation college graduates from families of modest means and little, if any, capital accumulation, simply do not have resources to support themselves in further graduate study. Also, many black students do not have the time and energy to do research, analyze data, and prepare a dissertation, while at the same time working full-time as professionals to support themselves and their families.

The argument often given by agents of philanthropic organizations is that universities should assume a greater role in financing graduate students as they progress in their courses of study. Such a position ignores the fact that racism has not been eradicated, root and branch, in the United States and that universities and other institutions in society are afflicted with this pathology. Thus, teaching and research assistantships, which are the traditional means of offering university support to advanced graduate students, are awarded first to majority-group students. This is because recommendations for such awards are usually the responsibility of faculty members, and few graduate faculties are sufficiently diversified to include a substantial number of black and other minority teachers. Minority graduate students seldom have mentors who fully understand their personal circumstances and who are willing to sponsor them and be their advocates in faculty councils where decisions on assistantships are made. The evidence indicates that mentors for black and other minority students are in short supply, especially in their schools of matriculation. Receiving limited nurturing and little support from university faculty contributes to the sense of isolation reportedly felt by some minority graduate students.

Not only does this study have important public policy implications, but it stands as a substantial contribution to social theory by way of the finding that students believe that a diversified student body results in a better race relations climate on campus. In terms of social theory, this finding suggests that intragroup and intergroup relations complement each other and are mutually influencing. In other words, knowledge, understanding, and interaction with people in one's own group may be enhanced through knowledge, understanding, and interaction with people in other groups.

With reference to human development theory, this finding may have implications for intrapersonal and interpersonal intelligence. One may come to know oneself better by coming to know others better. Thus, intrapersonal and interpersonal intelligences may be complementary and mutually enhancing too.

A graduate school student body that consists of all types of students is beneficial to whites as well as to racial and ethnic minority scholars: By coming to know others better, all may gain a better understanding of themselves. Thus, diversity on the college and university campus is its own reward.

APPENDIXES
REFERENCES
ABOUT THE AUTHORS
INDEX

Application Form
for Faculty Scholars

Period for which fellowship is requested: Check appropriate item:
   ___ Academic year, 19__ - 19__   ___ Initial applicant
   ___ Summer session(s), 19___   ___ Renewal applicant

      Mr.
1. Name: Ms._____
          First   Middle   Last

2. Date of birth: __/__/__   3. Telephone: (___)_____

4. Exact mailing address:_____
                                                                 zip code
5. Member of faculty at: _____Number of years: ____

6. Marital status: _____

   Number and relationship of dependents: _____

7. College and university training. List in chronological order all institutions
   attended even if credit was not earned. (Use extra paper, if necessary.)

   INSTITUTION   DATES   MAJOR   DEGREE

   _____

   _____

   _____

   _____

8. What foreign language do you read?_____

     With what facility? ___ Readily   ___ With difficulty

9. At what university do you plan to do graduate work or project?

   _____

10. Major field or project:_____

      Degree sought: 1. ___ PH. D.
                2. ___ ED. D.
                3. ___ Other (specify)_____

11. Estimate of funds needed for period of study:

a. Tuition & Fees $_____   e. Other expenses (please
                                                           itemize):
b. Living expenses   _____   _____ $_____
c. Travel & Relocation   _____   _____   _____
d. Books & Supplies   _____   _____   _____
e. Supplement for
      dependent children _____   _____   _____

                                   TOTAL $_____

12. List any distinctions received in scholarship or other areas such as writing,
    dramatics, athletics, etc.

    _____

    _____

    _____

13. Give names and addresses of three references (two references for renewals) at
    the graduate school where you are a candidate (or last graduate school
    attended), including department chairperson, professor in major field or the
    director of special project.

    _____

    _____

    _____

14. Beginning with your present position, list your professional employment history.
    Include for each position: your title, the name of the employing institution/
    agency, the name of your immediate supervisor, and the dates of employment.

    _____

    _____

    _____

    _____

    _____

    _____

PLEDGE: (To be signed by applicant)

    I pledge to return to the faculty of my UNCF institution for at least two
consecutive years immediately following my period of study under the Faculty
Fellowship Program.

Date:_____   Signature_____

Evaluation Questionnaire for College Presidents

1.   Name: _____ _____ _____
                       First   Middle   Last

2.   College with which you are affiliated:_____
_____

3.   Mailing address of school: _____
                              Street   City   State   Zip

4.   Your position:_____
                            Official title

5.   Check one:_____Chief Executive Officer _____Other Administrator

6.   (Fill in if not CEO) Name of Chief Executive Officer _____
_____

7.   Length of time in years you have been affiliated with this school:
_____

8.   Length of time in years in your present position: _____
_____

9.   Position held prior to the present appointment:_____
_____

10. Name and location of previous institution of appointment (if different
from current):_____
_____

11. List highest degree earned: _____ _____ _____
                                 Bachelor's Master's   Doctorate

11a. Institution from which highest degree was received: _____

12. Indicate whether you have an honorary doctorate: _____yes; _____no.

13. List your major field of study, on the job training, or the academic
discipline with which you identify:_____

A. General Information About School (1984-85 school year)

NOTE: If you do not have accurate data, please estimate

1. What is your school's official enrollment (f.t.e. or actual number)?

_____

2. What is your school's total budget (in dollars)?_____

3. How many full-time faculty do you employ?_____

3a. Of your full-time faculty, what percentage have doctorates?_____

3b. Of your full-time faculty, what percentage would you prefer to have

doctorates?_____

3c. Of all full-time members with doctorates, give number who used Lilly

assistance:_____ , don't know _____

4. Of your full-time faculty, what percentages fall into these

categories? (NOTE: Let your estimate add up to 100%)

Categories	Percent
Male	
Female	
Total	
Black	
White	
Other	
Total	
U.S. Citizen	
Foreign National	
Total	

5. Of your full-time faculty, what percentages in these categories do

and do not have doctorates? (NOTE: Let your estimate add up to 100%)

Categories	With Doctorates	Without Doctorates	Total
Male			
Female			
Black			
White			
Other			
U.S. Citizen			
Foreign National			

6. Is there pressure on your faculty members with doctoral degrees to accept employment elsewhere? _____yes; _____no.

6a. If yes, describe the extent of this pressure:

_____very strong; _____strong; _____moderate.

6b. If yes, indicate the principal sources of this pressure:

_____other colleges
_____government
_____business
_____social agencies
_____public elementary and secondary education
_____other

7. How many of your full-time faculty did not return to your college as employees in the 1984-85 school year? (Do not include faculty on leave.) _____

7a. What percentage of your total does this represent? _____

7b. Is the turnover rate in faculty for the past year typical of other years? yes_____ no_____

7c. If no, is it higher_____ or lower_____?

7d. During the past five years estimate the average turnover rate of full-time faculty in number - _____ and percentage - _____

8. Of faculty who did not return for the 1984-85 school year, where did they accept new positions (indicate number for each category)?

_____other UNCF colleges
_____other predominantly black public colleges
_____other predominantly white colleges
_____elementary or secondary education
_____city government
_____state government
_____federal government
_____business (corporation)
_____business (self-employed)
_____professional (self-employed)
_____church-related work
_____voluntary social service agency
_____homemaker
_____unemployed
_____do not know

B. Role of Faculty

    1. Rank these faculty functions from 1 as the most important to
10 as the least important:

Rank	Faculty Functions
	academic counseling of students
	attendance of professional conferences
	career counseling of students
	contact with alumni groups
	faculty advisor to student groups
	public service at local, state, and national level
	recruitment of new students
	research
	service on college committees
	teaching

    2. List other functions, if there are any not included above, that you
expect your faculty to perform (List in order of importance):

       a)_____

       b)_____

       c)_____

    3. Do you have a procedure for nominating Lilly/UNCF participants in
the faculty development program? _____yes; ____no.

   3a. If yes, what is it?_____

_____

_____

_____

   3b. If yes, what college official is responsible for nominations that
are forwarded to UNCF?_____

_____

   3c. If the president does not make the final nomination, what role does
he or she play?_____

_____

   3d. Can eligible faculty nominate themselves _____yes; _____no.

3e. Usually a participant in the Lilly/UNCF Faculty Development

Program is: _____ self-nominated
              _____ nominated by the college's procedure

4. Are there responsibilities at your school that you entrust only

to faculty with doctorate degrees? ____yes; ____no.

4a. If yes, what are these responsibilities and why are they reserved?

_____

_____

_____

_____

5. Do you have any expectations of your faculty members with doctorates

that differ from the expectations you have of faculty without

doctorates? _____yes; _____no.

5a. If yes, what are these? _____

_____

_____

_____

_____

6. How have faculty who have obtained their doctorates within the past

decade served your school in a way that enhances its educational

quality?_____

_____

_____

_____

_____

7. Do you consider assisting faculty to obtain doctoral degrees the

best way of enhancing the educational quality of your school?

_____ yes; _____no.

7a.   If no, what alternative approaches other than a faculty development
       program would strengthen the educational quality of your school?

       _____

       _____

       _____

       _____

7b.   What, in your judgement, is the strength of the Lilly/UNCF Faculty
       Development Program?_____

       _____

7c.   Is this a program that should be continued?   ____yes;   ____no.

7d.   If yes, should it be modified?_____

7e.   In your estimation, how might the Lilly/UNCF Faculty Development
       Program be modified to enhance the professional development of
       faculty at private black colleges?_____

       _____

8.   During the fellowship period, what level of contact does the
       institution maintain with its Lilly fellows?

       ___Monthly contact ___Contact several times a semester

       ___Annual contact ___No contact

8a.   What form does this contact take?_____

       _____

       _____

9.   What type of financial support, if any, does the college provide the
       Lilly fellow?

       ___Regular salary ___Living stipend ___Fringe benefits ___Other

       ___None

9a.   Amount of above support: _____

10.   Has the college with which you are affiliated participated in the Lilly/UNCF Faculty Development Program within the past ten years, or at anytime during your tenure as an administrative officer? ____yes; ____no.

10a. (Check whether your answer has to do with ____the full ten years, or ____the time that you have been an officer of your school)

10b. If no, explain why none of your school has applied for or been accepted as a Lilly/UNCF faculty fellow:_____

_____

_____

_____

_____

11.   Do you anticipate that any member or members of your faculty will apply to the Lilly/UNCF Faculty Development Program in the future? ____ yes; ____no.

11a. If yes, please estimate the number of faculty at your school who may be recommended during the 1985-86 school year.

_____
number

Questionnaire for Faculty Scholars

1. Name: _____
           (First)   Middle or   (Last)
                            Initial

2. College of employment: _____   3. _____
                              (Name)   (Number of years)

4. FILE code of college: _____
                       (Filled in by researchers)

5. Home mailing address: _____   _____
                       (No. and Street)   (City or Town and State)

   _____   6. _____   7. _____
    (Zip code)   (Home phone)   (Office phone)

8. Date of birth: _____   9. _____
                (Mo., Day, Year)   (Sex)

10. Race: _____   _____   _____
          (Black, foreign-born) (Black, USA-born)   (Hispanic)

    _____   _____   _____   _____
    Native American (Asian) (White) (Other - specify)

11. Family Status: _____   _____   _____   _____   _____
                (Married) (Legally-separated) (Divorced) (Widowed) (Single)

12. Number of years in above current family status: _____
                                          (years)

13. Offspring: _____
           (number)

14. Number of current dependents: _____   _____
                         (Offspring) (Other family)

15. Age of offspring (list from youngest to oldest now living) ___ ___ ___ ___
    ___ ___ ___ ___ ___

16. Place of birth: _____   _____   _____
                (Rural area) (Small town) (City)

17. State of birth: _____
                         (State)

18. Community in which most of childhood was spent

(a) _____ _____ _____ _____
     (rural) (small town) (city)   (state of birth)

(b) _____ _____ _____ _____
     (rural) (small town) (city)   (other than state of birth)

Educational and Occupational History of Parents and Spouse (if any)

Relation	Highest Level of Education Attained (check)					Usual or Highest Occupation Attained (check)						
	Elementary	High School	Col- lege	Grad. School	Home- maker	Labor- er	Service or Un- skilled Worker	Super- visor or Skilled Worker	Sales or Clerical	Mgr.	Prof.	
	1 2 3 4 5 6 7 8	9 10 11 12	1 2 3 4	1 2 3 4								
16. Mother												
17. Father												
18. Spouse												

16a. ____Do not have mother; 16b. ____Do not know mother's education;

16c ____Do not know mother's occupation.

17a. ____Do not have father; 17b. ____Do not know father's education;

17c. ____Do not know father's occupation.

18a. ____Do not have spouse.

19. Indicate the highest education attained by any sibling (brother or sister)
     in your family (circle)

     1 2 3 4 5 6 7 8   9 10 11 12   1 2 3 4   1 2 3 4
     Elementary   High School   College   Graduate School

20. Was the sibling who attained the highest education _____ or _____
                                                        (a brother)   (a sister)

21. Was the sibling who attained the highest education

     _____   _____
     (younger than you)   (older than you)

22. What is your ordinal position in your family:

     _____   _____   _____   _____
     (only child)   (oldest)   (youngest)   (between others)

23. Indicate the highest occupation attained by any sibling (brother or sister) in your family (check):

Homemaker	Laborer	Service or Unskilled	Supervisor or Skilled	Sales or Clerical	Mgr.	Professional

24. Was the sibling who attained the highest occupation: _____ _____
                                                         (a brother) (a sister)

25. Current position in school of employment (check): _____ _____
                                                      (lecturer) (instructor)

_____ _____ _____ _____ _____
asst. prof. assoc. prof. professor provost v.p., dean (or equivalent)

_____
other administrator

26. Current department (check): _____ _____ _____
                                social science education business adm.

_____ _____ _____ _____
mathematics and   humanities social work other - specify
natural science

27. Graduate record examination score: _____ or Miller Analogy score: _____
                                       (score)   (score)

28. Educational history (list undergraduate institution first)

Name of institution	State of institution	Period of Study Year to Year	Degree Earned	Date	Degree sought (if not earned)	Major Field of Study
a.						
b.						
c.						
d.						
e.						
f.						

28a. What is your current degree status (check):

_____ _____ _____
(taking courses)   (completed courses) (completed qualifying exam or paper)

_____ _____ _____
(writing dissertation) (completed dissertation) (received doctorate)

28b. In your judgment, the school from which you have or will receive your doctoral degree should be rated:

_____ _____ _____
(among the most selective (highly selective) (very selective)
in the country)

_____ _____
(selective) (not selective)

29. Source and level of financial support for doctoral study
(List in order initial and renewal grants separately, including Lilly
and other sources.)

Funding source of grant	Year	Point in program of study when grant was received (course work in years)									Qualifying Exam or Paper		Period of dissertation writing (years)				
		1st	2nd	3rd	4th	5th	6th	7th	8th	9th	Before	After	1st	2nd	3rd	4th	5th
a.																	
b.																	
c.																	
d.																	
e.																	
f.																	
g.																	

30. Employment history since college (list in order)

Organization of employment			Period of Employment	Estimated Annual Salary	Reasons for leaving					
Name	Type	State	Year to Year		Returned to school	Accepted another position	Illness or disability	Family relocation	Child rearing	Other
a.										
b.										
c.										
d.										
e.										
f.										
g.										
h.										
i.										
j.										
k.										

31. Scholarship record

Publishing history

Before receipt of doctoral degree	Number	After receipt of doctoral degree	Number
a. Articles			
b. Chapters in books			
c. Books			

Professional associations

Before doctorate	Number	After doctorate	Number
d. Membership in local ass'n			
e. Membership in state or regional ass'n			
f. Membership in national ass'n			

32. During the course of your study for the doctoral degree has anyone provided extraordinary support in the role of a mentor ___yes, ___no

33. If yes, was this individual: ___at your school of employment
                                   ___at your doctoral institution
                                   ___at your undergraduate institution
                                   ___other (specify)

34. If yes, how many years have you known your mentor _____

35. If yes, is your mentor: ___male
                              ___female

36. If yes, is your mentor: ___black
                              ___white
                              ___other (specify)

37. If yes, what is the field of specialization of your mentor: _____

38. If no, what was your feeling about the value of a mentor:

     ____did not need a mentor
     ___did not want a mentor
     ___wanted a mentor but never had one

39. In general, how did you feel about the following experiences at your doctoral institution. (Please check one category for each experience.)

Feeling

Personal Experience of Campus Life	Very Satisfied	Satisfied	Dissatisfied	Very Dissatisfied	No Opinion
a. The general competence of the administration					
b. Availability of study space on campus					
c. Quality of housing					
d. Safety and security of campus environment					
e. Health services					
f. Recreational facilities					
g. Library service					
h. Food service					
i. The general competence of the faculty					
j. Quality of instruction					
k. Contact with faculty outside of class					
l. Accessibility of advisor					
m. Accessibility of faculty on dissertation committee					
n. Evaluation of student assignments and examinations					
o. Opportunity to collaborate with faculty in research and writing					
p. Opportunity to relate to faculty of own race or ethnicity					
q. Racial and ethnic diversity of faculty					
r. Diversity of faculty in gender					
s. The general competence of the student body					
t. Friendliness of students					
u. Opportunity to participate in student study groups					
v. Participation in graduate student organizations					
w. Opportunity for joint participation in recreational activities					
x. Racial or ethnic diversity of student body					
y. Opportunity to relate to students of own race or ethnicity					
z. Race relations climate on campus					
aa. Leadership among graduate students on campus					
bb. Opportunity to meet members of local community					
cc. Opportunity to serve as teaching assistant					
dd. Opportunity to serve as research assistant					
ee. Availability of financial aid					

40. What was your cumulative grade point average when you finished college _____

41. Check the category that best represents your overall academic performance in college: __A, __A-, __B+, __B, __B-, __C+, __C, __C-, __D+, __D

42. What is your cumulative grade point average for your doctoral studies: _____

43. Check the category that best represents your overall academic performance in doctoral study: __A, __A-, __B+, __B, __B-, __C+, __C, __C-, __D+, __D

44. In general, did you work while in school studying for the doctoral degree _____   _____
                                              (yes)   (no)

45. Approximately how many hours per week did you work while studying for your graduate degree _____
                                              (hours)

46. Did you receive any financial support from your school, while you were studying for your graduate degree _____   _____
                                                            (yes)   (no)

47. If yes, what form did this support take   _____
                                               (regular salary)

   _____   _____
   (partial salary)   (fringe benefits)

48. Upon completion of your doctoral degree, what are your plans for employment in the future:

    ___plan to return to current school for two years only

    ___plan to return to current school for five years only

    ___plan to return to current school for ten or more years

    ___plan to return to current school but prefer immediate employment elsewhere

    ___do not plan to return to current school

49. Do you plan to complete studies and receive your doctorate _____   _____
                                                              (yes)   (no)

50. If yes, in which year do you intend to graduate _____
                                                     (year)

51. If no, what has interfered with the completion of your studies
    for the doctorate

    ___job responsibilities

    ___family responsibilities

    ___dissatisfied with doctoral program

    ___career change

    ___too old

    ___illness or disability

    ___other (specify)

52. After you receive your degree, do you expect to be appointed to a
    different position from your current post ____ ____
                                               (yes) (no)

53. If yes, what position would you prefer _____

54. If you have already received your doctoral degree, has your role
    in your current institution changed ____ ____
                                         (yes) (no)

55. If yes, have you been promoted to one of the following positions:

    ___assistant professor

    ___associate professor

    ___professor

    ___department chair

    ___division head

    ___administrator other than V.P., Dean, Provost, President

    ___dean

    ___vice president

    ___provost

    ___equivalent rank of VP, Dean, Provost

    ___President

56. Before completing your doctoral degree which of the following positions did you last occupy:

___assistant professor

___associate professor

___professor

___department chair

___division head

___administrator   other than V.P., Dean, Provost, President

___dean

___vice president

___provost

___equivalent rank of VP, Dean, Provost

___president

57. In general, how, if at all, has the UNCF-Lilly Endowment Faculty Development Program enhanced your ability as a teacher and scholar:

_____
(greatly enhanced skills)

_____
(enhanced skills)

_____
(moderately enhanced skills)

_____
(has not enhanced skills)

58. In your opinion would you have been able to complete your doctoral degree without assistance from the UNCF-Lilly Endowment Fund

        ____   ____
        Yes   No

59. How might the current UNCF-Lilly Program be modified to more effectively contribute to faculty development for staff in UNCF schools (base answer on your own experience or that of others whom you know):   _____

_____

_____

_____

References

Abatso, Yvonne. 1987. Coping strategies: Retaining black students in college. In Anne S. Pruitt (Ed.), *In pursuit of equality in higher education* (pp. 123–131). Dix Hills, NY: General Hall.

Allen, Walter R. 1986. *Gender and campus race differences in black student academic performance, racial attitudes, and college satisfaction.* Atlanta: Southern Education Foundation.

Allen, Walter R. 1981. Correlates of black student adjustment, achievement, and aspirations at a predominantly white southern university. In Gail E. Thomas (Ed.), *Black students in higher education* (pp. 126–141). Westport, CT: Greenwood Press.

Astin, Alexander. 1982. *Minorities in higher education.* San Francisco: Jossey-Bass.

Astin, Helen S., & Cross, Patricia H. 1981. Black students in black and white institutions. In Gail E. Thomas (Ed.), *Black students in higher education* (pp. 30–45). Westport, CT: Greenwood Press.

Blackwell, James E. 1987. *Mainstreaming outsiders* (2nd ed.). Dix Hills, NY: General Hall.

Blackwell, James E. 1983. *Networking and mentoring: A study of cross-generational experiences of blacks in graduate and professional schools.* Atlanta: Southern Education Foundation.

Boyd, W. M. 1974. *Desegregating America's colleges.* New York: Praeger.

Brown, Darryl. 1986, February. Do black colleges have a role in the '80s? *Youth Policy,* pp. 6–8.

Browning, Jane E. Smith, & Williams, John B. 1978. History and goals of black institutions of higher learning. In Charles V. Willie & Ronald R. Edmonds (Eds.), *Black colleges in America* (pp. 68–93). New York: Teachers College Press.

Carter, Deborah, & Wilson, Reginald. 1989. *Eighth annual status report: Minorities in higher education.* Washington, DC: American Council on Education.

Cross, Patricia H., & Astin, Helen S. 1981. Factors affecting black students persistence in college. In Gail E. Thomas (Ed.), *Black students in higher education* (pp. 76–90). Westport, CT: Greenwood Press.

Fleming, Jacqueline. 1984. *Blacks in college.* San Francisco: Jossey-Bass.

Fleming, Jacqueline. 1975. *Motivational determinants of bi-racial competition in black male college students.* Unpublished manuscript, Radcliffe Institute, Cambridge, MA.

Franklin, John Hope. 1967. *From slavery to freedom* (3rd ed.). New York: Knopf.

Gibbs, J. T. 1974. Patterns of adaptation among black students at a predominantly white university. *American Journal of Orthopsychiatry, 44*, 728–740.

Gurin, P., & Epps, E. G. 1975. *Black consciousness, identity and achievement*. New York: Wiley.

Hartnett, Rodney, & Payton, Benjamin F. 1977. *Minority admissions and performance in graduate study*. New York: Ford Foundation.

Jones, B. A. 1974. The tradition of sociology teaching in black colleges: The unheralded profession. In J. E. Blackwell & M. Janowitz (Eds.), *Black sociologists* (pp. 121–163). Chicago: University of Chicago Press.

Leighton, Alexander H. 1946. *The governing of men*. Princeton, NJ: Princeton University Press.

Levinson, Daniel J. 1978. *The seasons of a man's life*. New York: Ballantine.

McGrath, E. G. 1965. *The predominantly Negro colleges and universities in transition*. New York: Teachers College Press.

Monro, John. 1978. Teaching and learning English. In Charles V. Willie & Ronald R. Edmonds (Eds.), *Black colleges in America* (pp. 235–260). New York: Teachers College Press.

Morgan, James & Associates. 1962. *Income and welfare in the United States*. New York: McGraw-Hill.

National Center for Educational Statistics. 1989a. *The condition of education, 1989: Vol. 1. Elementary and secondary education*. Washington, DC: U.S. Government Printing Office.

National Center for Educational Statistics. 1989b. *The condition of education, 1989: Vol. 2. Postsecondary education*. Washington, DC: U.S. Government Printing Office.

National Center for Educational Statistics. 1989c. *Digest of educational statistics, 1989*. Washington, DC: U.S. Government Printing Office.

National Center for Educational Statistics. 1988a. *Digest of educational statistics, 1988*. Washington, DC: U.S. Government Printing Office.

National Center for Educational Statistics. 1988b. *Youth indicators, 1988*. Washington, DC: U.S. Government Printing Office.

Nettles, Michael T. 1988. *Toward black undergraduate student equality in higher education*. Westport, CT: Greenwood Press.

O'Brien, Eileen. 1989, September 28. Some gains, some losses in minority test scores. *Black Issues in Higher Education, 6*, 1, 12–13.

O'Neil, R. M. 1975. *Discriminating against discrimination: Preferential admissions and the DeFunis case*. Bloomington: Indiana University Press.

Patterson, Frederick D. 1943, January 30. *Pittsburgh Courier*.

Rockefeller Foundation. 1977. *Fellowship programs: Preparing minority group members for educational leadership*. New York: Rockefeller Foundation Publications Office.

Scott, Gloria R. 1981. The economic future: Institutional and student financial aid for blacks in higher education. In Gail E. Thomas (Ed.), *Black students in higher education* (pp. 357–379). Westport, CT: Greenwood Press.

Thomas, Gail E. 1987. Black college students and their major field of choice. In Anne S. Pruitt (Ed.), *In pursuit of equality in higher education* (pp. 105–115). Dix Hills, NY: General Hall.

Thomas, Gail E. 1981. Conclusion. In Gail E. Thomas (Ed.), *Black students in higher education* (pp. 381–390). Westport, CT: Greenwood Press.

Thompson, Daniel. 1973. *Private black colleges at the crossroads.* Westport, CT: Greenwood Press.

Tollett, K. S. 1978, January/February. What led to *Bakke? The Center Magazine*, pp. 2–10.

Trent, William T., & Copeland, Elaine. 1988. The production of black doctoral recipients: A description of five states' progress. In John Williams (Ed.), *Desegregating America's colleges and universities: Title VI regulation of higher education* (pp. 54–70). New York: Teachers College Press.

U.S. Bureau of the Census. 1980. *Social indicators III.* Washington, DC: U.S. Government Printing Office.

Upton, James N., & Pruitt, Anne S. 1985. *Financial assistance to black doctoral students in two Adams' states: A policy analysis.* Atlanta: Southern Education Foundation.

Willie, Charles V. 1989a. Blacks, A valuable national pool of talent. In Wornie Reed (Ed.), *Assessment of the status of African Americans: Summary* (pp. 1–17). Boston: University of Massachusetts, William Monroe Trotter Institute.

Willie, Charles V. 1989b. *Caste and class controversy on race and poverty: Round two of the Willie/Wilson debate.* Dix Hills, NY: General Hall.

Willie, Charles V. 1987. *Effective education.* Westport, CT: Greenwood Press.

Willie, Charles V. 1986. *Five black scholars.* Lanham, MD: University Press of America and Abt Books.

Willie, Charles V., & Cunnigen, Donald. 1981. Black students in higher education. *Annual Review of Sociology, 7,* 177–198.

Willie, Charles V., & Edmonds, Ronald R. (Eds.). 1978. *Black colleges in America.* New York: Teachers College Press.

Willie, Charles V.; Grady, Michael K.; & Hope, Richard O. 1985. *Faculty development program for private black colleges: An evaluation* (A report). Cambridge, MA: Harvard University, Graduate School of Education.

Willie, Charles V., & MacLeish, Marlene. 1978. The priorities of presidents of black colleges. In Charles V. Willie & Ronald R. Edmonds (Eds.), *Black colleges in America* (pp. 132–148). New York: Teachers College Press.

Willie, Charles V., & McCord, Arline. 1972. *Black students at white colleges.* New York: Praeger.

Wilson, William Julius. 1987. *The truly disadvantaged.* Chicago: University of Chicago Press.

Wolters, R. 1975. *The new Negro on campus: Black college rebellions of the 1920s.* Princeton, NJ: Princeton University Press.

About the Authors

Charles V. Willie is Professor of Education and Urban Studies, Graduate School of Education, Harvard University. He is former President of the Eastern Sociological Society and was appointed by President Jimmy Carter to the President's Commission on Mental Health. He co-directed the Black College Conference at Harvard University in 1976 and co-edited *Black Colleges in America* (Teachers College Press, 1978). Dr. Willie received a Bachelor of Arts from Morehouse College in 1948, a Master of Arts from Atlanta University in 1949, and a Ph.D. from Syracuse University in 1957.

Michael K. Grady is Director of Research and Evaluation for the Prince George's County Public Schools, Maryland. Current research projects being conducted in the school system include studies on black male achievement, compensatory education, site-based management, and computer-assisted instruction. Prior to his work in Prince George's County, Dr. Grady participated in the development of a long-range plan for magnet schools in St. Louis. His recent publications are in the area of minority student achievement, educational equity, and the politics of education. Dr. Grady received his master's and doctoral degrees in educational administration, research, and policy analysis from the Harvard Graduate School of Education.

Richard O. Hope is currently Vice President of the Woodrow Wilson National Fellowship Foundation. He helped to prepare the report *Education That Works: An Action Plan for the Education of Minorities* as the Executive Director of the Quality Education for Minorities Project at the Massachusetts Institute of Technology. For a decade and a half, Dr. Hope served as chairperson and professor in the sociology departments of Morgan State University and Indiana University at Indianapolis. While working as an assistant professor of sociology at Brooklyn College, he was Research Associate with Kenneth B. Clark at the Metropolitan Applied Research Center, where he conducted studies of the public schools of Harlem, New York, which concluded in the HARYOU (Harlem Youth Opportunity Unlimited) Study. Dr. Hope is a graduate of Morehouse College in Atlanta, Georgia, and received his Ph.D. in sociology at Syracuse University's Maxwell School of Citizenship and Public Affairs.

Index

Note: *Italicized* page numbers indicate material in tables

Abatso, Yvonne, 24
Academic record
  of black students, 5–6
  of faculty scholars, 30–31, 45–46,
    73–74, 80–81
Achievement tests, 11
Admissions process
  academic competence and, 5–6
  financial aid and, 3–5
Advisors, 78–79
Affirmative action, 25–26
African-Americans
  academic competence of, 5–6
  college enrollment trends among,
    1–3
  effects of financial aid policies on,
    3–5
  first college graduates, 1
  importance of Ph.D. degree for, 19
Allen, Walter R., 24, 50–51
American Council on Education, 3–4
Ashmun Institute, 1
Astin, Alexander, 23, 25, 27, 51
Astin, Helen S., 50, 51
Atlanta University, 13, 43

Black colleges and universities, 8–18
  adaptation of black scholars to,
    53–57
  civil rights movement and, 9–11
  earliest, 1, 8–9
  faculties of, 9–10, *15*, 16–18
  nonblack schools vs., 23–25
  persistence of students and, 10–11,
    23, 25, 46

problems of, 11
  as supportive communities, 10–11,
    23–24
  United Negro College Fund (UNCF)
    and, 12–18
  use of, by faculty scholars, 42–43
  vocational vs. liberal arts education
    in, 8–9
  See also specific colleges and
    universities
Black Issues in Higher Education,
  5
Blacks. *See* African-Americans
Black Students at White Colleges
  (Willie & McCord), 71
Blackwell, James E., 1, 2, 6, 25–27,
  66, 70–72
Boyd, W. M., 23
Brown, Darryl, 17–18
Browning, James E. Smith, 8
Brown v. *Board of Education*, 2

Carter, Deborah, 3–5
Citicorp, 17
Civil Rights Act of 1964, 10
Civil rights movement, 9–11
Civil War, 8
College Board, Scholastic Aptitude
  Test (SAT), 5
Commission on the Higher Education
  of Minorities, 27
Copeland, Elaine, 25–26
Cross, Patricia H., 50, 51
Cunnigen, Donald, 25
Currier, T. S., 67, 72

111

Hartnett, Rodney, 51–52
Harvard College, 1
Harvard University, 1
Higher Education Act, Title III, 3, 17–18
Hope, Richard O., 20
Howard University, 2
Humanities, 44–45, 81

Jones, Butler A., 10

King, Martin Luther, Jr., 2, 3

Leighton, Alexander H., 25
Leovinger, 24
Levinson, Daniel J., 27, 67
Lilly Endowment/UNCF Faculty
    Development Program
  academic record of scholars in,
      30–31, 45–46, 73–74, 80–81
  degree status of faculty scholars in,
      28–30, 73–74
  employment of participants in,
      36–39, 41, 46–47, 74, 77, 81
  evaluation study of, 20–23
  fields of study of scholars in,
      44–45
  financial support systems and,
      36–39, 74, 75, 77–78, 81–82
  location of doctoral programs in,
      42–43
  mentoring relationships and, 67–72,
      78–79, 82
  occupational history of participants
      in, 46–47
  origins of, 16–18
  payback requirements for
      participants, 75–76
  personal and family background of
      participants in, 31–36, 82
  post-fellowship experience of
      participants in, 47–49
  purposes of, 23
  questionnaire for college presidents
      and, 21, 89–95

questionnaire for faculty scholars
    and, 21–22, 96–104
survey of faculty scholars in, 20–23,
    87–88
Lincoln University, 1

MacLeish, Marlene, 10–11
Mainstreaming Outsiders (Blackwell),
    70
Marital status, *32, 33*
Mathematics, 19–20, 45, 81
Mays, Benjamin, 10
McCord, Arline, 24, 25, 71
McGrath, Earl G., 10
Medical college admissions, 6
Meharry Medical College, 2
Mellon Foundation, 17
Mentors, 27, 52, 67–72, 78–79, 82
  characteristics of, *69*
  functions of, 67–68
  prevalence of student relationships
      with, 68
  selection process and, 68–70
  See also Faculty
Minority groups
  college dropout rates for, 23
  population growth of, 81
Monro, John, 11
Morehouse College, 9
Morgan, James and Associates, 35
Morrill Act, 8
Motivation, 46

National Association for the
    Advancement of Colored People
    (NAACP), 2
National Center for Educational
    Statistics, 2–7
Nettles, Michael T., 24

O'Brien, Eileen, 5
O'Neil, R. M., 25

Parents, education of faculty
    scholars', 34–36